Don DeLillo's
Underworld

CONTINUUM CONTEMPORARIES

· **DON DeLILLO'S**

Underworld

A READER'S GUIDE

JOHN DUVALL

CONTINUUM | NEW YORK | LONDON

2002

The Continuum International Publishing Group Inc
370 Lexington Avenue, New York, NY 10017

The Continuum International Publishing Group Ltd
The Tower Building, 11 York Road, London SE1 7NX

www.continuumbooks.com

Printed in the United States of America

Library of Congress Cataloging-in-Publication Data

Duvall, John N. (John Noel), 1956-
 Don DeLillo's Underworld : a reader's guide / John Duvall.
  p. cm. — (Continuum contemporaries)
 Includes bibliographical references (p.   ).
 ISBN 0-8264-5241-8 (pbk. : alk. paper)
 1. DeLillo, Don. Underworld.   I. Title. II. Series.
PS3554.E4425 U5334 2002
813'.54—dc21   2001047383

Contents

Acknowledgements

Conversations with Theron Britt and Paul Naylor helped shed light on many of the dark corners in *Underworld*. Thanks for your insights and friendship. And to my wife, Kathy Schroth, what can I say? She knows where my obsessions dwell.

Portions of Chapter 2 draw on my essay "Baseball as Aesthetic Ideology: Cold War History, Race, and DeLillo's 'Pafko at the Wall,'" which appeared in *Modern Fiction Studies* (Summer 1995). An expanded version of this essay was reprinted in *Critical Essays on Don DeLillo* (G. K. Hall, 2000), edited by Hugh Ruppersburg and Tim Engles. My thanks to these editors and publishers for permission to use this material here.

1

The Novelist

BACKGROUNDS

In the spring of 1999, the announcement came from Israel
that Don DeLillo had won the Jerusalem Prize. The award, given
every two years since 1963, honors a writer whose body of work
expresses the theme of the individual's freedom in society. On June
23, 1999, he was honored in a ceremony at the Jerusalem International Book Fair. As the first American recipient of the award,
DeLillo joins an international group of distinguished novelists, play-
wrights, and philosophers that includes Bertrand Russell, Simone
de Beauvoir, Jorge Luis Borges, Eugene Ionesco, V. S. Naipaul,
Milan Kundera, and Mario Vargas Llosa. In selecting DeLillo, the
jury characterized his work as "an unrelenting struggle against even
the most sophisticated forms of repression of individual and public
freedom during the last half century" (19th Jerusalem). The prize
signals the canonical status DeLillo's work has begun to achieve in
the last decade. DeLillo, in fact, has established himself as one of
the leading American candidates for the Nobel Prize for Literature.

Winning this prize, though, may prove more difficult, since the Nobel usually is given to those authors who write about the human heart in conflict with itself and not to one such as DeLillo who so directly challenges the legitimacy of multinational capitalism and its manipulation of the image through media and advertising to construct first-world identity via the individual's acts of consumption. In *Underworld*, however, DeLillo may have succeeded in wedding his cultural critique to characters with fully developed inner lives that recall an older novelistic sense of the human heart.

Whether DeLillo eventually wins the Nobel, his lasting place in American literature at present seems certain, an unlikely achievement for someone who started life as the child of Italian immigrant parents. (DeLillo's father came to America in 1916 when he was nine years old and eventually worked his way up to a position as an auditor for a life insurance company.) Born on November 20, 1936 in New York, Donald Richard DeLillo experienced an ethnic childhood in a working-class North Bronx neighborhood. Yet after his apprentice short stories of the 1960s, any representation of his ethnicity simply drops out of his fiction from *Americana* (1971) through *Mao II* (1991). As one critic noted in 1990, DeLillo's "name could just as well be Don Smith or Don Brown" since there's "nothing particularly 'ethnic' about his dark comedy" (Aaron 68). It is precisely DeLillo's recovery of his ethnic roots that marks *Underworld* as his most personal work to date. As DeLillo notes, it was only in reading the galleys for *Underworld*, with its representation of 1950s Italian-American Bronx life, that he realized he was "reliving experience" through his central character, Nick Shay (whose mother reverts to her Irish maiden name after his father, Jimmy Costanza, disappears), "in a curious and totally unintentional way"; elaborating, DeLillo says,

When I first started writing I wrote short fiction, short stories set mostly in [the Bronx] and when I finally got to work on my first novel, *Americana*—the title itself says something—this was a kind of journey into the broader culture. A curious unintentional form of repetition of my own parents' journey, my immigrant parents who came to the U.S. from Italy. This was their way out of a certain narrowness, an economic narrowness, into a country that promised certain things.

When I was in my early 20s maybe that background and those narrow streets seemed to be a bit constricting in terms of what I could get out of them as a writer because I hadn't yet developed a perspective, a maturity as a writer. (Echlin)

DeLillo's comments, in which he effectively claims his maturity as a writer, allow a new perspective from which to see his earlier life. His repeated use of the word "unintentional" in relation to *Underworld* underscores the fact this novel contains more autobiographical elements than any of his previous fiction. In addition to the character Nick Shay, Albert Bronzini also serves as an angle of vision that allows DeLillo to recapture the neighborhood of his youth. Bronzini, the artist manqué, who even thinks "walking was an art" (661), strolls through the Italian neighborhood in the opening chapter of Part 6, processing the details of the street scenes with a finely honed aesthetic consciousness.

Catholicism was a part of DeLillo's Italian-American upbringing, an aspect he has acknowledged: "I think there is a sense of last things in my work that probably comes from a Catholic childhood. For a Catholic, nothing is too important to discuss or think about, because he's raised with the idea that he will die any minute now and that if he doesn't live his life in a certain way this death is simply an introduction to an eternity of pain" (Passaro, "Dangerous"). Despite Catholicism's looming threat of eternal damnation, DeLillo was drawn to Church rituals, such as high funeral masses, calling them some of his "warmest childhood memories"; moreover, DeLillo sees a link between religious ritual and art; he notes that Catholic "ritual had elements of art to it and it prompted feelings that art sometimes draws out of us. I think I reacted to it the way I react today to theater." (LeClair, 26).

In the early 1950s, DeLillo would later discover, he lived just a half dozen blocks from his near contemporary, Lee Harvey Oswald. Although the two never met, this proximity inspired DeLillo to write his ninth novel, *Libra* (1988), a novel that challenges the Warren Commission Report's assertion that Oswald acted alone in assassinating President Kennedy. After graduating form Cardinal Hayes High School in the Bronx, DeLillo attended Fordham University, a Jesuit institution, from 1954 to 1958 earning a B.A. in "something called communication arts." At Fordam, DeLillo claims, "the Jesuits taught [him] to be a failed ascetic" (Harris). (In *Underworld*, Nick Shay, after attending reform school run by Jesuits, attends a college in rural Minnesota that is an experimental satellite program administered by Fordam.)

In 1959, DeLillo took a position as a copywriter for Ogilvy and Mather, an advertising agency. This work experience finds expression in *Underworld*'s portrayal of Madison Avenue office culture in Chapter 2 (the "December 19, 1961" fragment) of Part 5, where we see Charles Wainwright's soul-killing work of constructing aesthetically pleasing misrepresentations of orange juice. While working for Ogilvy and Mather, DeLillo began to write fiction. His first published story, "The River Jordan," appeared in *Epoch* in 1960. By 1964, DeLillo had his fill of corporate American and quit his job to become a freelance writer. Recalling this time, DeLillo says, "I did all sorts of assignments. One day I would be writing about pseudo-colonial furniture, the next day about computers." (Goldstein, 56). Such assignments supplied barely enough income to pay the rent on a studio apartment in the Murray Hill section of New York while he continued to publish the occasional short story in various literary magazines. As a struggling young writer, DeLillo lived a spartan existence, earning only around $2000 a year. In 1966 he began work on what would become his first novel, *Americana*, which is dedicated to Barbara Bennett, whom he would marry in 1975. (The couple is still married.) With the publication of this novel, DeLillo leaves behind his freelancing to devote himself to his fiction.

DeLILLO'S FICTION AND *UNDERWORLD*

Underworld, DeLillo's post-mortem on American Cold-War paranoia, serves as a culmination of many of the themes, concerns, and ideas of his earlier fiction written during the Cold War. Despite being DeLillo's first novel, *Americana* in some respects may be the closest to *Underworld* in terms of a broad scope through which the author attempts to understand American identity in relation to media and consumer culture. In both novels, a male protagonist seeks authenticity: in *Americana* it is a young man, David Bell, who runs away from his position as a television executive to find himself, while in *Underworld*, it is an older man, Nick Shay, who races off into the desert in search of a lost self.

Long before *Underworld*, DeLillo had taken up the threat of nuclear annihilation in his second novel, *End Zone* (1972), an allegorical novel in which college football players embody various philosophical positions and which meditates on the connections between the language of football and that of nuclear war. In *Great Jones Street* (1973), DeLillo returns to the effect of the media. When rock star Bucky Wonderlick attempts to leave his band in mid-tour in order to recover some sense of a private self, his star status only grows, fueled by a media hungry for celebrity content, and he helplessly becomes a more public figure.

DeLillo's next novel is the dense and difficult Menippean satire, *Ratner's Star* (1976), in which fourteen-year-old mathematical genius Billy Twilig joins a secret underground think tank. This collection of eccentric scientists, who see but dimly any connections between their research and its possible applications, seems to anticipate DeLillo's portrayal of the work of *Underworld*'s "bombheads," who are similarly secreted in a wasteland underground and are charged with developing newer, better designs for nuclear weaponry; they don't necessarily love war but they do love the challenge of the science. Both novels' underground scientists thematize DeLillo's suspicion of America's military-industrial complex.

DeLillo's next two novels, focusing on conspiracy and paranoia, show his darkening view of contemporary America. *Players* (1977) looks the marriage of Lyle and Pammy Wynant as it becomes implicated in various undergrounds. Lyle has an affair with a terrorist who draws him into her world, and Pammy interposes herself as the third in the life of a gay male couple with disastrous results. In *Running Dog* (1978) DeLillo speculates about America's interest in the life of Adolph Hitler as a way of suggesting the latent fascist impulses in American culture. The novel's plot centers on a race between reporters and intelligence agents to find a purported pornographic film that Hitler made during the final days of the Führer bunker. At the same time, evidence emerges of conspiracy within the CIA to do freelance work — agents who use their surveillance equipment to kill for hire.

As interesting, thoughtful, and funny as these early satiric novels are, DeLillo might only have become a footnote in literary history, overshadowed by Thomas Pynchon's examinations of American paranoia, if it weren't for the work DeLillo has done in since the 1980s. A turning point occurs when DeLillo receives a Guggenheim Fellowship in 1979 and travels to Greece where he remains for the next three years. In the summer of 1988, DeLillo acknowledges the change, claiming "the novels I've written in the 1980s . . . were more deeply motivated and required a stronger sense of commitment than some of the books I wrote earlier . . ." (DeCurtis, 65). His time in Greece and India provides DeLillo the setting for *The Names* (1982). In this novel James Axton, an American risk analyst living in Greece, stumbles onto the existence of an ancient death cult that murders victims by matching their initials with the place of their death. But despite the trappings of the thriller that DeLillo had deployed in his two previous novels, *The Names* is about language and the possibility of meaning.

DeLillo's time in Greece proved equally important for the new purchase it gave him on America. Without his travel abroad, his eighth novel, *White Noise* (1985) might never have been written. As DeLillo puts it:

When I came back to this country in 1982, I began to notice something on television which I hadn't noticed before. This was the daily toxic spill — there was the news, the weather, and the toxic spill. This was a phenomenon no one even mentioned. It was simply a television reality. It's only the people who were themselves involved who seemed to be affected by them. No one even talked about them. This was one of the motivating forces of *White Noise.* (Rothstein)

The ecological threat of chemical pollutants and the power of capitalism, through television and advertising, to normalize — indeed to render invisible — this threat is a theme that *Underworld* expands and develops. *White Noise* also continues DeLillo's examination of proto-fascist impules in American culture through its first-person narrator, Jack Gladney, the middle-aged chair of the Department of Hitler Studies at a small midwestern liberal arts college.

Clearly *White Noise*, which won the National Book Award, represents a turning point in DeLillo's reputation. Prior to the award, a relatively small number of mostly academic readers had admired the author. But with *White Noise* and its scenes of blended family life, DeLillo finds a larger audience. Additionally, the novel finds a place in the university and is now one of the most frequently taught exemplars of postmodernism.

Since the acclaim of *White Noise*, DeLillo has muted an element that had formed a significant part of his earlier fiction—the overt satire of American culture. Although the critique of postmodern America continues in *Libra, Mao II*, and *Underworld*, it does so in a from that Linda Hutcheon has termed "historiographic metafiction." For Hutcheon, the postmodern novel blends the reflexivity of metafiction (fiction that calls attention to itself as fiction or fiction that thematizes its own fictional production) with an explicit questioning of what counts as official history. Historiographic metafiction intentionally and self-consciously blurs the boundary between history and fiction, a move that makes explicit what traditional historiography wishes to obscure—that any attempt to write history involves interpretive moments that implicate the historian in gestures indistinguishable from those of novel writers. For Hutcheon, the contemporary novel's blend of history and fiction creates a purchase for postmodern parody and for an art with the potential to comment critically on the culture of which it is nevertheless inescapably a part.

Libra, then, takes up a moment that DeLillo sees as crucial to the history of the twentieth century, the assassination of President John F. Kennedy. The chapters alternate between a fairly straightforward biography of Kennedy's assassin, Lee Harvey Oswald, and the narration of a CIA analyst, Nicholas Branch. Branch's role metafictionally doubles DeLillo's, for the character has been charged with writing a report that makes sense of the assassination. Supplied by the CIA archivist with ever more bits of textual evidence, Branch discovers the gaps and silences of the Warren Commission Report. Elsewhere DeLillo has called this official report of what happen in Dallas, Texas, "the novel that James Joyce might have written if he had moved to Iowa City and lived to be a hundred" (DeCurtis, 53–54).

DeLillo has long been fascinated with crowds and people's collective urge to be a part of something larger than themselves, to surrender to a power that would explain the felt alienation of their lives and to protect them from a recognition of their own mortality. *Mao II* with its frightening evocations of crowds both in text and image—a mass wedding ceremony performed by Reverend Moon at Yankee Stadium, the suffocation of people pressed against a restraining fence at a soccer match, and the mass hysteria at the Ayatollah Khomeini's funeral—can be read in relation to DeLillo's representation of a thoroughly American crowd at the baseball game that opens *Underworld*. More important, though, is DeLillo's concern in *Mao II* for what remains of the possibility of the novel as a medium to affect social consciousness. The main character is the reclusive novelist Bill Gray, an individual who wishes to keep details of his life a secret. Like Bucky Wonderlick, though, Gray discovers that the more he seeks privacy the more he becomes the object of public and academic interest. It is tempting to see parallels between Bill Gray and DeLillo, an author who until the publication of *Underworld* was well-known for guarding his private live. (He famously once handed an interviewer a business card that said, "I don't want to talk about it"). Gray, who has stopped writing, is uncertain that there is any vocation left for the contemporary novelist: "There's a curious knot," he claims, "that binds novelists and terrorists. . . . Years ago I used to think it was possible for a novelist to alter the inner life of the culture. Now bomb-makers and gunmen have taken that territory. They make raids on human consciousness. What writers used to do before we were all incorporated" (41). Although it would be overly simplistic to equate DeLillo with

Bill Gray, a character actually modeled on both Thomas Pynchon and Salman Rushdie, DeLillo spoke in 1991 about the relation between narrative and terrorism:

> In a repressive society, a writer can be deeply influential, but in a society that's filled with glut and repetition and endless consumption, the act of terror may be the only meaningful act. People who are in power make their arrangements in secret, largely as a way of maintaining and furthering that power. People who are powerless make an open theater of violence. True terror is a language and a vision. There is a deep narrative structure to terrorist acts, and they infiltrate and alter consciousness in ways that writers used to aspire to. (Passaro, "Dangerous")

I have written at some length about *Mao II* because I believe one can read *Underworld* as DeLillo's attempt to write a contemporary novel that would recover the potential for fiction to infiltrate and alter consciousness in an American society of endless consumption.

LITERARY AND INTELLECTUAL INFLUENCES

In addition to his Roman Catholic upbringing that I noted earlier, DeLillo attributes a portion of his authorial identity to the city in which he was raised: "I think New York itself was an enormous influence. The paintings in the Museum of Modern Art, the music at the Jazz Gallery and the Village Vanguard, the movies of Fellini and Godard and Howard Hawkes" (Harris). And certainly *Underworld* depicts both art and film in a specifically New York setting.

DeLillo has responded several times over the years to the inevitable question about his literary influences. In 1982 he tells Thomas LeClair, "Probably the movies of Jean-Luc Godard had a more immediate effect on my early work than anything I'd ever read"

(25). The authors he acknowledges as influences (Vladimir Nabokov, James Joyce, Hermann Broch, Malcolm Lowery, and William Faulkner) are canonical high and late modernists: "The books I remember and come back to seem to be ones that demonstrate the possibilities of fiction. *Pale Fire, Ulysses, The Death of Virgil, Under the Volcano, The Sound and the Fury*—these come to mind. There's a drive and daring that goes beyond technical invention."(26). Responding ten years later to Adam Begley, DeLillo mentions some of his early reading, noting that James T. Farrell's *Studs Lonigan* trilogy "showed me that my own life, or something like it could be the subject of a writer's life." Then when he was 18, he read while working as a parking lot attendant: "And this is where I read Faulkner, *As I Lay Dying* and *Light in August*. And got paid for it. And then James Joyce, and it was through Joyce that I learned to see something in language that carried a radiance, something that made me feel the beauty and fervor of words, the sense that a word has a life and a history." Herman Melville and Ernest Hemingway, DeLillo notes, also raised his awareness of language (278).

Despite his personal sense that the modernists serve as his main influences, DeLillo is most often compared to such contemporaries of his as Thomas Pynchon and William Gaddis who almost seem to form a school of American postmodern satirists. And *Underworld*, as we shall see, alludes fairly directly to Pynchon's *The Crying of Lot 49* and *Gravity's Rainbow*. But it is equally useful to see DeLillo in relation to other historiographic metafictionists—novelists who blur the boundary between history and fiction and who see the novel as writing a kind of underground history. Seen in this fashion, E.L. Doctorow's *The Book of Daniel* (1971) and *Ragtime* (1974) both seem to point to the kind of work DeLillo does in *Underworld*. Doctorow's highly metafictional *Book of Daniel*, a fictional telling of the Rosenberg executions, is in fact a history of the shift from old left in America and the emergence of the new left in the anti-

Vietman War movement. And *Ragtime* examines myths of American national identity in the early part of the twentieth century. In the later novel, Doctorow's mix of fictional characters with fictionalized versions of historical figures (such as Harry Houdini, Henry Ford, J. P. Morgan, and Emma Goldman) prefigures a strategy DeLillo deploys in *Underworld* in which Russ Hodges, J. Edgar Hoover, Frank Sinatra, and Lenny Bruce all appear as characters. Moreover, Doctorow's oft-stated sense of the novel's duty to question official versions of history dovetails closely with DeLillo's purpose in *Underworld*. In fact, DeLillo's essay, "The Power of History," which appeared in *The New York Times Magazine* a month prior to the publication of *Underworld* and which details the genesis of this novel, casts the novel as a genre in the role of providing a counter-history to official history. He explicitly compares his use of Hoover in underworld to Robert Coover's use of Richard Nixon as a narrator in *The Public Burning* (1977), another fictional retelling of the executions of Julius and Ethel Rosenberg for selling atomic secrets. DeLillo also commends *Ragtime* for the way its language creates a "version of the past that escapes the coils of established history and biography" (63). Considered as a historiographic metafictionist, DeLillo may have as much in common with Toni Morrison, whose novel *Beloved* (1987) refigures the tragedy of Margaret Garner through the character of Sethe Garner in order to tell the hidden history of slavery, as he does with the high postmodernists with whom he is most often grouped.

Not all of DeLillo's influences are filmic or novelistic, however. His eclectic reading shows a familiarity with contemporary issues in social theory that have been crucial in academic discussions of postmodernism. Reading DeLillo's fiction one encounters casual references to such figures as the Marxist literary and cultural theorist Herbert Marcuse and reads cultural analyses eerily resonant with those of the French social theorist Jean Baudrillard.

From *White Noise* on, DeLillo has examined American mass culture's desire to find transcendence through such things as television, consumption, and crowd behavior. A shorthand term for this desire for an almost religious transcendence is aura. In an interview, DeLillo has admitted to a familiarity with "The Work of Art in the Age of Mechanical Reproduction," the famous essay on aura by the Frankfurt School critic Walter Benjamin. Aura for Benjamin is a negative concept because it cloaks the work of art in its cultic and ritual function (225–26). Benjamin speaks approvingly of the way new technologies of mass reproduction destroy the aura of the high culture work of art that fetishizes origin: if high quality prints of the *Mona Lisa* can be infinitely reproduced and disseminated, it is no longer necessary to travel to the Louvre and stand in hushed respect before timeless genius. He hoped that film and photography could recuperate aura in a Marxist sense that would politicize the aesthetic; however, in the epilogue of his essay, Benjamin, a firsthand observer of Hitler's National Socialists, notices that in the Nazi appropriation of culture, it is not just art but the media "which is pressed into the production of ritual values" (243). Far from simply destroying aura, the techniques of reproduction (particularly the newly emerging electronic media) could reconstruct a specious aura. If Hitler could construct an aura by using newsreels and radio to amplify the impact of his parades, rallies, and sporting events, then there was a link between mass reproduction and the manipulation of the masses (253) For Benjamin, then, one of the defining features of fascism is its ability to transform political conflict and class struggle into objects of aesthetic contemplation.

In one of his most influential essays, "The Order of Simulacra," Jean Baudrillard continues the discussion of aura. Starting from Benjamin and Marshal McLuhan, Baudrillard shifts away from a Marxist analysis of technology as a productive force toward an interpretation of technology "as medium" or expressive form (99). Taken to is extreme, McLuhan's "the medium is the message" becomes Baudrillard's hyperreal, where the "contradiction between the real and the imaginary is effaced" (142). Baudrillard's sense of postmodernity resonates with that of the American Marxist theorist Fredric Jameson. For Jameson, postmodernism can only be the cultural logic of multinational capitalism. Such a position radically diminishes the possibility of an oppositional aesthetic. In fact, for Jameson, all contemporary aesthetic production has been subsumed by commodity production. In simpler terms, what this means is that the amount of time between the emergence of a new aesthetic form (such as rap music) and its appropriation by Madison Avenue to sell everything from fast food to running shoes has been so radically reduced that the ability of that new aesthetic form to create a critical purchase on the social order has been thoroughly undercut. Thus the dialectic of DeLillo's fiction in general and of *Underworld* particularly plays out between Jameson's pessimistic view of postmodernism (one that certainly sees no vocation for the historical novel) and Hutcheon's more optimistic sense that sees the postmodern historiographic novel as opening a space of implicated social critique. With pessimism of the intellect but optimism of the spirit, DeLillo continues to write novels that probe American postmodernity.

2

The Novel

"What's a ball game to make us feel like this?
PROLOGUE, *UNDERWORLD*

MATTER AND SCOPE

Despite the fact that DeLillo is most frequently cast as a postmodern novelist, *Underworld*'s method of presenting its story of memory and desire recalls the chronological disruptions of modernist narration. DeLillo himself has noted as much; while allowing that many of his earlier novels could be identified as postmodern, he says, "I don't see *Underworld* as post-modern. Maybe it's the last modernist gasp" (Williams). One way to think of DeLillo's relation to postmodernism is by an analogy to a modernist American author, F. Scott Fitzgerald. Although not as formally inventive as James Joyce or William Faulkner, Fitzgerald wrote about modernity—the impact of the new in industrial society—automobiles, telephones, jazz recordings. Similarly one might say of DeLillo that he does not hit the high notes of ludic style or press the boundaries of representation as does Thomas Pynchon or Donald Barthelme; nevertheless, DeLillo's subject matter has always been postmodernity—what it feels like to live in the contemporary moment.

Underworld is nothing short of an attempt to account for the emergence of paranoia as a significant feature of American national identity during the Cold War. This is also, then, a novel about how the United States became postmodern, both culturally and aesthetically. The US victory over the Soviet Union, DeLillo's novel suggests, was achieved not entirely by the official governmental policy of the containment of communism. In its failure in the hot war with Vietnam, United States excesses—saturation bombing, the use of Agent Orange to defoliate the countryside, and terrorism directed against civilians—in retrospect clearly seem to have bolstered the resolve of the North Vietnamese. Instead, *Underworld* posits that America won the Cold War in large part because, in the classic economic metaphor, it was able to have both guns and butter—both a strong military presence abroad and a proliferation of consumer goods at home. The Soviet Union may have been able to match US nuclear tonnage, but not its consumerism. *Underworld* at one point represents this 1950s consumerism in a satirical set piece on an archetypal American nuclear family, the Demings, whose lives are surrounded by new things and whose world picture is shaped by new words "to believe in and live by":

Breezeway	Car pools
Crisper	Bridge parties
Sectional	Broadloom (520)

There is, however, an underside to this brave new world. While dad is in the driveway waxing the family's new two-tone Ford and mom is in the kitchen making her Jell-O chicken mousse, son Eric sits "in his room, behind drawn fiberglass curtains, jerking off into a condom. He liked using a condom because it had a sleek metallic shimmer, like his favorite weapons system, the Honest John, a surface-to-surface missile with a warhead that carried yields up to forty tons" (514). That evening, father and son plan to take the binoculars and drive into the country to see if they can catch a glimpse of the Soviet's recently launched satellite, Sputnik.

This consumer culture represented by the Demings is crucially linked to capitalism's control of the image through saturation advertising on all forms of the electronic media (radio, television, film, and, today, the World Wide Web). The hidden costs of American consumer culture are observable in a national identity shaped by the Cold War's master Us-Them binary—the United States versus the Soviet Union. A fundamental binarism, *Underworld* suggests, became mirrored even in massive political movements in the 1960s that questioned America's master narrative of good and evil: the Civil Rights movement read racial politics in terms of black and white, and the anti-Vietnam war protest polarized opponents and supporters of the war, often along what was termed the "generation gap."

At the same time, *Underworld* considers what happens to American identity when this stable ground of belief is suddenly removed in the aftermath of the Cold War. As Marvin Lundy, DeLillo's historian manqué, puts it: "You need the leaders of both sides to keep the cold war going. It's the one constant thing. It's honest, it's dependable. Because when the tension and rivalry come to an end, that's when your worst nightmares begin. All the power and intimidation of the state will seep out of your personal bloodstream" (170). The Cold War effectively masked the political economy but in its aftermath, nothing covers over the rapaciousness of multinational capital. The threat of nuclear apocalypse may have receded, but, *Underworld* warns, with little to contain capitalism's colonization of global markets, an environmental apocalypse looms.

The body of Underworld covers a forty year period from 1951 and a crucial moment in Cold War history through the period following the break-up of the Soviet Union, though the epilogue's concluding scenes of web surfing seem to bring us much nearer to the novel's publication date in 1997. Geographically, the novel takes us from New York and Boston through the midwest of Wisconsin and Minnesota to the desert Southwest and the west coast (Los Angeles and San Francisco) and finally to the Kazakhstan weapons test site in the former Soviet Union.

Against this world political stage, we see the effects of both consumer and radioactive waste on the lives of particular people. If T. S. Eliot's Waste Land describes the spiritual malaise of post-World War I modernity, DeLillo attempts to diagnose through its pre-history the spiritual disconnectedness of post-Cold War post-modernity. Like Eliot, DeLillo uses a literal wasteland — the recurring representation of massive landfills — to figure spiritually wasted lives. His very title, Underworld, takes us in many directions. Nick Shay always suspects that his father, Jimmy Costanza, a small-time numbers runner who disappeared suddenly, was killed by the criminal underworld. DeLillo's characters also encounter artist renderings of the underworld, from apocalyptic representations such as The Triumph of Death (which gives DeLillo's prologue its title) by 16th century painter Pieter Bruegel to a screening of Unterwelt, a supposedly lost silent film of Russian director Sergei Eisenstein. The novel's characters, who live in the recent American past, inevitably experience these earlier artistic visions as a foreshadowing of nuclear annihilation. But the most persistent meaning of underworld is the volume of waste generated by American consumer culture. DeLillo claims to have decided on the title when thinking of plutonium waste buried in the desert Southwest. While meditating on the word he recognized the link to "Pluto, the god of the dead and ruler of the underworld," which allowed connections of all sorts, particularly to "the underhistory of the Cold War, a curious history of waste which forms an underground stream in this book, waste and weapons" (Echlin). If an archeology of Cold War America is ever to be performed, the novel suggests, it must take place in the massive landfills near our urban areas. DeLillo argues that, perhaps as much as the proliferation of nuclear weapons, the proliferation of consumerism and disposable goods was a key weapon in American's Cold War arsenal. Even as he makes explicit the link between nuclear and consumer waste, DeLillo represents yet another underworld, the homeless of New York City, who fall outside of American consumerism and thus give the lie to the cornerstone assumption of American ideology — that we are a classless society.

STORY AND STRUCTURE

Underworld records Nick Shay's modernist search for lost time. The novel's structure is unusual in that it juxtaposes a backward and a forward presentation of time. Because of this double movement, the plot of the novel is paradoxically quite different than the story of the characters' lives. That is, since so many things are plotted in reverse chronological order, the things we don't know about characters create plot tensions that simply would disappear if one were to retell the story by reconstructing a conventional timeframe.

For example, when we meet Nick in part 1, we know his end. In 1992 he is 57-year-old executive for a waste management company in Phoenix, Arizona. Although a successful executive and family man, he is suddenly seized with an identity crisis. In part he has a dawning awareness that his wife, Marian, is having an affair with their good friend, Brian Glassic. More significant, though, is Nick's sense that he lives like someone in a witness protection program; in this regard, Nick is a postmodern Everyman who represents so many people who in their adult lives live and work far from their childhood homes. But Nick makes a performance of his alienation, amusing coworkers with his impersonations of a mafioso godfather. What precipitates Nick's crisis of identity is his reading a story about a woman with whom he had a brief affair forty years ago, Klara Sax, and her work on a giant outdoor art installation. Renting a car, he drives into the desert ostensibly to find Klara but in fact in quest of what he takes to be a lost authenticity—a sense of himself as someone who was at one time whole and complete and a part of community. That time of imagined completeness is his youth growing up in an Italian-American neighbor of the Bronx; as Nick puts it in his final words of the novel: "I long for the days of disorder. I want them back, the days when I was alive on the earth, rippling in the quick of my skin, heedless and real. I was dumb-muscled and angry and real. This is what I long for, the breach of peace, the days of disarray when I walked real streets and did things slap-bang and felt angry and ready all the time, a danger to others and a distant mystery to myself" (810). But Nick's sense of his earlier identity as authentic, in the larger structure of the novel, is simply misinformed, since that earlier identity is the historically specific construction of the cultural logic of the Cold War.

Nick's youth is full of intimations of a criminal underworld. Over and above his suspicions regarding his father's disappearance, Nick is haunted throughout the novel by a youthful act, shooting a friend, which lands him in the juvenile correction system. As this plot unravels in reverse chronology, then, the climax of the novel is when we discover that Nick's crime is an ambiguous one. He does kill an older man, the shadowy and reclusive George Manza, with a sawed off shotgun, but Nick does not really intend to kill George. Nick, in fact, is drawn to George, who serves a kind of surrogate father figure, albeit a dark and troubled one, suggesting various underworlds of his own. Nick, who fancies himself a young tough, is merely a rebel without a cause. At one point George, a heroin addict, offers heroin to Nick. At their next meeting, George shows his sawed-off shotgun to Nick. In an impulsive moment, Nick points the gun at George. George tells Nick that the gun is not loaded and to pull the trigger. Nick accepts the gambit and blows George's head off. Seeing this moment finally represented in Part 6 answers the reader's question—what is Nick's crime? The mystery of Nick's previous broodings about being dangerous and violent are cast in a new light when we see that his "crime" is more accidental than intentional. In retrospect, one can see why Nick criminalizes his killing of George. Because Nick believes his father to be the victim of a mob hit, he transforms the accident of killing George, a father substitute, into a spectral and guilty intent, which reveals Nick's unconscious sense that he is responsible for the disappearance of his biological father, Jimmy Costanza. Nick is, in his underground psychic life, the hit man who wastes the Father imago.

If, however, we were to turn the narrative around and retell the story of Nick's life, his killing George, (rather than the narrative's climax,) would be nearer its beginning because this act, which doubles Nick's loss of the father, jolts Nick out of the banality of his life as a day laborer, whose recreation is shooting pool and engaging in casual sex, and leads to a more socially engaged life through the interventions of reform school and the Jesuit college he then attends.

Klara Sax, Nick's partner in the adulterous relationship, is a major character, but not the main focus. When we meet her in Part 1, she is at peace with herself and engaged in the culminating work of her long artistic career. For Klara, the 1952 affair with Nick awakens her from the complacency of her role as a middle-class wife and mother and gives her the courage to leave the family and pursue a career as an artist. For Nick, the moment completes the oedipal drama. At 34, Klara, who is twice Nick's age, is strongly associated with the concept of motherhood—as the mother of a daughter and in her apprentice appreciation of the formal realism of Whistler (a copy of Whistler's mother "watches" Nick and Klara's sexual intercourse.) Her husband, Albert Bronzini, is another displaced father/authority figure, as a high school math teach and the chess mentor of Nick's younger brother, Matt. In sum, Nick at these symbolic removes does kill the Father and have sex with the Mother. Klara's identity crisis, far from any oedipal scenario resulting from the affair with Nick, occurs in Part 4 when she is 54-years-old during the summer of 1974. Having achieved a certain standing in the New York art world, she experiences a fallow period and must reassess her aesthetic. Passing this crisis she is able to return to her work.

There are many other stories in *Underworld*, but for the most part they revolve around the couple involved in the affair. Matt Shay, a chess prodigy in his youth, goes on to serve in the Vietnam war and later to work in an underground facility that hones nuclear weapons technology. Part 4 juxtaposes as Klara's aesthetic crisis with Matt's ethical crisis as he tries to come to terms with his doubts about the value of his work. The novel also records the changes that happen to Bronzini. In Part 6 he appears as a man happily married to Klara, but in Part 2 we see him as an elderly man caring for his sister afflicted with Alzthiemers.

Although this provides a general outline of *Underworld's* story, the novel itself is crucially framed by a prologue that brilliantly constructs a crucial historical context. This context suggests how apparently unrelated events in the story (such as Nick and Klara's affair and Nick's shooting George) participate in an underground historical logic. The prologue allows us to see how, when the Soviet Union became America's Cold War other, all Americans became, figuratively speaking, secret agents.

THE PROLOGUE AND
ITS RELATION TO NOVELISTIC STRUCTURE

Set at the Polo Grounds on October 3, 1951, the prologue retells
the events of one of baseball's most memorialized moments, the
third and deciding playoff game for the National League champi-
onship between two New York teams, the Dodgers and the Giants.
The game is famous for Bobby Thomson's "Shot Heard 'Round the
World," a ninth-inning, two-out, three-run home run that gives the
Giants the pennant. Even though none of the novel's central characters are introduced in this 50-page piece (which was published as
a novella under the title "Pafko at the Wall" in the October 1992
issue of *Harper's*), the multiple perspectives on the baseball game
establish many significant concerns of the novel. The prologue
examines baseball as an aesthetic ideology that participates in mask-
ing the hidden costs of America's Cold War victory and in erasing
race and class difference. One technique DeLillo uses to structure
his novel is to trace the history of the ball Thomson hit through its
various owners. Nick, the current owner of the ball, has a pro-
foundly personal stake in the game. As a Dodgers fan, the defeat
marks a kind of loss of faith; the larger political context of this day
shapes not only his but all the characters' identities in subtle yet
profound ways.

   At its simplest level, the prologue serves as a moment of origin,
both of the history of the baseball Thomson hit and of the Cold
War. If the novel proper moves from the present to the past, the
prologue begins a linear narrative that reveals the history of the
baseball from the time it is recovered in the stands to its first sale.
This immediate history of the ball appears in the prologue and
three subsequent chapters, each titled "Manx Martin," that are
positioned between the novel's major divisions; these interludes

occur between Parts 1 and 2, between Parts 3 and 4, and finally between Parts 5 and 6. The prologue and these interludes represent the missing twelve hours in the ball's history, hours that are unknowable to even the most dedicated investigation by Marvin Lundy, a baseball memorabilist, throughout the rest of the novel. As DeLillo tells Kim Echlin, "these two conflicting streams" — the linear and reversed chronology narratives — "lock together because on the day after [Manx Martin] sells the baseball, Part Six begins."

Clearly DeLillo uses the Giants-Dodgers rivalry to figure a different and larger Us-Them opposition. If a New Yorker's identity (at least for those who were not loyal to the Yankees) in the early 1950s could be read in part based on whether that individual was a Dodgers' or a Giants' fan, then American identity more fully in that same period is shaped in its opposition to the Soviet Union. DeLillo later uses the Dodgers-Giants rivalry to register the strangeness of living in the aftermath of the Cold War. In 1992 Nick attends a business dinner at a restaurant in Dodger stadium in Los Angeles. Unlike the immediacy of the raucous New York crowd of the prologue, a glass wall now separates Nick and his dinning companions from the crowd watching the Dodgers play the San Francisco Giants. Both the United States-Russia and the Dodgers-Giants oppositions mean something very different in 1992 than in 1951. Old loyalties and beliefs are rendered archaic. Just as the Dodgers and the Giants left New York to tap into the lucrative West Coast market, so too have market forces rewritten the relation between America and Russia.

What makes clear the metaphorical relationship between baseball fans' identification with their teams and American identity is the historical significance of this date in history that DeLillo explores. On this day, the Soviet Union exploded their second atomic weapon, a fact that confirms for US intelligence that the Soviets had nuclear capability. In *Underworld* DeLillo explores a massive irony: if America remembers October 3, 1951, it is for the Thomson home run and not for its significance in Cold War history. Yet the confirmation of Soviet nuclear capability meant that the United States then had an adversary powerful enough to sustain post-WWII paranoia about threats to America's sovereignty. Beginning with this last moment of postwar confidence in our exclusive possession of nuclear weapons, DeLillo sets the stage for his examination of American history from the 1950s to the early 1990s and this history's effect on his characters.

In DeLillo's portrayal of American consumer culture, he repeatedly finds political and economic matters overwhelmed by aesthetics. It is precisely baseball fans' auratic identification with the game that DeLillo makes problematic as it raises a question: Why on a particular day in our history—October 3, 1951—does one cultural event, a baseball game, eclipse a moment crucial to the construction of the Cold War? *Underworld* evokes American nostalgia about baseball and the early 1950s in order to critique both, and it is this critical evocation of nostalgia that allows the novel to double as a commentary on post-Cold War American life and the ways it is implicated in authoritarian—indeed almost proto-fascist—urges.

OCTOBER 3, 1951: BASEBALL AND AURA

In *Underworld*, DeLillo unpacks much of the ideological baggage surrounding America's game. The action of the prologue is perceived mainly from three alternating angles of vision, each of which serves to show how baseball's auratic function masks crucial political realities: from the announcer's booth comes the self-reflexive thoughts of a historical figure, Russ Hodges, the radio voice of the Giants, as he broadcasts the game; in Leo Durocher's box seats, three cultural icons—Jackie Gleason, Frank Sinatra, and J. Edgar

Hoover—watch the game with famous New York barman Toots Shor; and, far removed from the announcer's booth and the box seats, a fourteen-year-old African-American youth watches the game from the left field seats. All three strands work together to show how baseball serves in popular culture a function equivalent to T.S. Eliot's high-culture tradition: baseball, like Eliot's poetic tradition, is an aestheticized space that allows the reader/viewer to experience a sense of transcendence, a removal into a realm of the timeless and universal; in short, like Eliot's tradition, baseball's tradition is ahistorical, an ideal order that any particular game must refigure if it is to enter the tradition.

DeLillo plays the odd grouping of Shor, Gleason, Sinatra, and Hoover simultaneously for comic and nostalgic effects: between rounds of beer, Gleason pleases surrounding fans by doing bits from his new television show, *The Honeymooners*, that would air for the first time two nights later; Hoover worries that Gleason will start teasing him about being short. Their presence at the game might be ludicrous—a bit of postmodern excess—if there were not much about the grouping that is plausible, especially regarding Hoover, who initially seems most anomalous in the group. In "The Power of History," an essay that appeared shortly before the publication of *Underworld*, DeLillo in fact claims that he learned that the "four-some had been present at the ballgame" (62).

Despite the humor surrounding this group, it is the introduction of Hoover that allows the novel to comment on the way global politics become aestheticized, so much so that the history of the Cold War nearly disappears from American consciousness. DeLillo draws our attention to this when an FBI agent brings Hoover the news of the Soviet Union's detonation of a second atomic device. The novel is historically accurate on this point, and DeLillo has spoken about the "sense of history" he experienced in his discovery of the front page of the October 4th edition of the *New York Times*, which bears a dual headline: the left side telling of Bobby Thomson's home run; the right side, in typeface of the same pitch, announcing the Russian atomic bomb. ("Power" 60). We have, it seems, a tale of two blasts — Bobby Thomson's three-run blast and the Russian atomic blast. The Russian blast will give Hoover the "ammunition" to pursue even more fully his anti-Communist agenda, for it is this second explosion that confirms Russian nuclear capability. It is hardly an exaggeration to say that on this day the Cold War becomes fully viable. Yet in American consciousness, Cold War history is overwhelmed by baseball legend.

Each of the major angles of vision on the game is represented at the moment of Ralph Branca's home run pitch to Thomson; Hoover's perspective, however, is particularly noteworthy for its engagement with the aesthetic past. In the shower of paper falling from the stands, a page from *Life* magazine falls on Hoover's shoulder which then catches his eye as he starts to brush it off. It is a color reproduction of Bruegel's *The Triumph of Death*; this "landscape of visionary havoc and ruin" becomes the object of extended close study for Hoover as time seems to slow while Thomson rounds the bases:

It covers the page completely and must surely dominate the magazine. Across the red-brown earth, skeleton armies on the march. Men impaled on lances, hung from gibbets, drawn on spoked wheels fixed to the top of bare trees, bodies open to the crows. Legions of the dead forming behind shields made of coffin lids. (41)

Even after Thomson has scored and the fans pour onto the field, Hoover still contemplates "the meat-blood-colors and massed bodies," which become in his mind a figuration of nuclear apocalypse. Looking up from Bruegel's images, Hoover sees the confusion and moiling of celebrants on the field, and they become indistinguishable to him from the ravaged sinners he has been scrutinizing on the page.

Hoover is an apt figure for DeLillo's consideration of proto-fascist impulses in American culture. In *White Noise*, if Professor Jack Gladney, Chair of the Department of Hitler Studies, teaches a course in "the continuing mass appeal of fascist tyranny" (25), it is because DeLillo himself is the real student of the subject. In 1951, Hoover was the chief of what amounted to a kinder, gentler American Gestapo, a secret police with almost unchecked power to use electronic surveillance to spy on American citizens. It may be useful to note here the third major story on the front page of the *New York Times* the day after the big game: under the headline of the Giants' win is a photo of Leo Durocher hugging Bobby Thomson; balancing the page, under the headline of the Soviet blast is a photo of Philip Jessup denying Senator Joseph McCarthy's charges of communist sympathies at a Senate Foreign Relations subcommittee. The Dodgers-Giants game is played a year and half after McCarthy's famous charges about the 205 Communists working in the State Department. McCarthy's biggest problem, of course, was that he had no list and so turned to Hoover, a friend since he arrived in Washington in 1947, for help in keeping the issue alive. McCarthy became a media star, but Hoover made it happen by supplying the Senator with embarrassing information about individuals, often illegally obtained and consisting largely of gossip and rumor too insubstantial for the Justice Department to act on (Gentry, 377–382).

Although Hoover is a relatively minor character in the novel as a whole, he does reappear in Part 5. In an episode from November 1966, DeLillo explores the fallout from the America policy of the containment of communism—the Vietnam War and the protest at home against the war. These scenes have Hoover attending Truman Capote's Black and White Ball, a mix of celebrity in all walks of political, artistic, and sporting life. DeLillo emphasizes particularly Hoover's well-known, long-time personal relationship with Clyde Tolson, Hoover's top aid at the FBI. Recent biographical work strongly implies Hoover's homosexuality, but in DeLillo's telling, despite a clear homoeroticism between Hoover and Tolson, Hoover is celibate. His celibacy and refusal to act on his sexual urges in fact is central to his power over others, a power that frequently turned on Hoover's uncovering others' sexual behaviors. Imagining a celibate Hoover allows DeLillo to parallel J. Edgar Hoover to another character, Sister Alma Edgar, a Catholic nun, who is as obsessed with ferreting out sin as Hoover is with uncovering the secrets of those under his surveillance. Both are anal and paranoid, deeply fearing germs and the contamination from crowds. Just as Hoover is a crucial perspective in the prologue, Sister Edgar is integral to the novel's epilogue, a point I will return to later.

BASEBALL AND RACE

If *Underworld* illustrates the dangerous tendency of baseball to aestheticize and erase international politics, it also comments on the way that baseball can participate in a mystification of racial politics within America. Against the fame and aura of the celebrities the prologue portrays, there is the anonymity of Cotter Martin, a black member of the underclass, who along with a crowd of other black and white teenagers jumps the gates to get into the Polo Grounds for the big game. The novel in fact opens with Cotter: "He speaks in your voice, American, and there's a shine in his eye that's halfway hopeful" (11). By beginning his novel with a focus on this African-American youth, DeLillo signals that American identity is in fact constituted by what it marks as the culturally abject; the racial Other, in other words, is crucial to rather than separate from such identity. (The name "Cotter Martin," in fact, seems a barely concealed anagram for Cotton Mather [1663–1728], the Puritan theologian and historian who envisioned a very exclu-

sive American identity in *Magnalia Christi Americana*.) Cotter is
marked by an American ideology of equality and justice, even if he
has not experienced them directly; despite his blackness, he is "halfway hopeful." Cotter, quite simply, believes in baseball and to
believe in baseball is to believe in America. In part, this belief
comes from his home life. His older sister, Rosie, in 1964 travels
from New York to participate in a Civil Rights protest in Jackson,
Mississippi. The event turns violent when the National Guard gas
and beat the crowd, which includes "white nuns marching with
black ministers" (523). Even as things begin to turn ugly, the
speaker who has been exhorting the marchers onward tells them in
a deeply ironic moment: "I'm saying there's nothing in the world to
worry about despite the evidence all around you. Because anytime
you see black and white together you know they are joined in some
effort of betterment. Says so in the Constitution" (524). The vio-
lence of this later moment of failed interracial cooperation shatters
the innocence of the mixed race crowd of youthful gate jumpers at
the ballgame who work together to defeat the stadium cops with
their nightsticks.

Yet much about the way Cotter is delineated marks his racial
and class status. After he has found a seat in the left-field stands, he
is made conscious of his race by a flashy peanut vendor who deftly
catches the coins people toss his way:

It's a thrill-a-minute show but Cotter feels an obscure danger here. The guy is
making him visible, shaming him in his prowler's den. Isn't it strange how
their common color jumps the space between them? Nobody saw Cotter until
the vendor appeared, black rays phasing from his hands. One popular Negro
and crowd pleaser. One shifty kid trying not to be noticed. (20)

One person who notices Cotter is Bill Waterson, a middle-aged
white architect. Bill recognizes Cotter as a gatecrasher from his

nervousness yet engages the youth in conversation, and they start to recognize a shared experience; both have taken the day off (from school, from work) to watch the big game. Realizing they are both Giants fans, Bill and Cotter develop a friendship over the course of the game, an ostensible bonding between two males who can appreciate individually talented players within baseball's larger tradition. Cotter's racial and class identity, through Bill's big-brotherly attention, seems to melt away as the game wears on.

When the baseball Thomson hits breaks the plane of the outfield wall giving the Giants victory, however, we leave the space of fictionalized history and enter historicized fiction. The illusion of a timeless aesthetic space in which racial differences don't matter dissolves as Cotter and Bill scramble to recover the ball Thomson hit. In the scuffle, Cotter wrests the ball from someone who he moments later realizes is Bill. This struggle over the white ball also takes on overtones of the white domination of the sport in 1951, a domination that was soon to end. Although the color bar in the major leagues officially had been broken by Jackie Robinson in 1947, African American players in this game — Robinson, Willie Mays, and Roy Campanella — are as much interlopers on the field as Cotter Martin is in the stands.

Bill pursues Cotter for many blocks — arguing, pleading, cajoling. Bill offers to buy the ball, but when Cotter won't sell the ball, baseball's position as the great Americanizer unravels. Bill, like Cotter, believes in baseball, but from the subject position of a middle-class white male, Bill's belief means something different than Cotter's. And what Bill believes neatly summarizes the American ideology of baseball:

I look at you scrunched up in your seat and I thought I'd found a pal. This is a baseball fan, I thought, not some delinquent in the streets. You seem dead set on disappointing me. Cotter? Buddies sit down together and work things out. . . . Now tell me what it's going to take to separate you from that baseball, son. (56)

Baseball, Bill knows, is supposed to build better boys, and the understanding he hopes for, of course, is that Cotter will recognize the white man's property interest in the ball. When Cotter asserts that "the ball's not yours, it's mine" (56), Bill's condescendingly avuncular tone ceases and the chase begins in earnest, as Bill with increasing rage pursues the youth until they reach Harlem, when the middle-aged man now realizes he sticks out as much as Cotter had in the ballpark.

What Bill fails to realize is the contradictory nature of his belief that baseball can ensure the stability of the status quo — of middle-class property interests at home and of America as a world super-power. If baseball is supposed to save kids from the mean streets of the city, what happens if the American lessons the game is supposed to teach (courage, independence, and risk-taking) are transferred from the playing field to the streets? Quite simply, a black youth can challenge a white man over property.

Although Cotter Martin fades from the novel after the prologue, DeLillo continues his mediation on the impact of race in three chapter-length sections that fall between major divisions of the novel. Taken together, they form a coherent linear narrative that focuses on the immediate fate of the Thomson ball, from Cotter's return home on October 3, 1951, to the sale of the ball by his father, Manx, early the next morning to a fan waiting in line to buy World Series tickets. In the first of these sections, Cotter, who needs a note to explain his absence from school, tells his father about the game and the ball. Manx, as a bit of a con man and the father of an impoverished family, immediately sees the potential to sell the ball. Although Cotter does not want to sell the ball, Manx takes it when his son falls asleep. The remaining two sections record Manx's efforts to sell the ball.

It is in the sale of the ball that DeLillo reiterates the ideological function of baseball to mask race and class difference. After being rebuffed by several people — for even Manx knows he sounds fraudulent since he has no way to document his claim that he has the Thomson ball — Manx discovers a father and son, Charles (Chuck) and Chuckie Wainwright, in the ticket line. In the course of the deal, Manx and the other man, Chuck, emphasize what is common between them — particularly their fatherhood. However everything in the encounter is racialized. For example, Chuck is persuaded by the logic that Manx, as an African-American, would not be believed by the Giants' management if he showed up at their offices to sell them the ball. And at a key moment in the deal, when Chuck passes his whiskey flask to Manx, Manx must wait to see whether Chuck will wipe the rim before drinking again.

Early in the novel the reader learns that Nick Shay, the current owner of the Thomson ball, paid $34,500 for the memento, despite the missing link in the lineage of the ball — every owner of the ball is known back to October 4, 1951, but no connection to the original owner can be made. Manx sells the ball — and surely his son's trust — for $32.45. Manx's betrayal of Cotter mirrors Nick's sense of loss in his relation to his father and points to an unconscious motive for Nick's eventual purchase of the Thomson ball. For Nick, the uncertainty about the authenticity of the baseball he owns functions as a displaced representation of a more primal unknowability — the true reason for his father's disappearance. In sum, the ball for Nick (and in many ways for the novel itself) is a fetish object that compensates for losses, both public and private.

MEDIA AND THE POSTMODERN

If the treatment of Hoover's and Cotter's perspectives create a critical purchase on the historical past, then DeLillo's presentation of the radio announcer, Russ Hodges, serves to make the critique relevant to our equally historical present. Hodges is clearly an artist figure, who contemplates the constructive nature of his discourse. His presence shows that even in DeLillo's evocation of a more innocent America, the country was already becoming postmodern in its relation to the electronic media. We see through Hodges a world in which the model of reality will precede and generate the real. Prior to the game he recalls his father's taking him to the Dempsey-Willard fight in Toledo; what he takes as a "measure of the awesome" is clearly made so for him by its media representation: "When you see a thing like that [fight], a thing that becomes a newsreel, you begin to feel you are a carrier of some solemn scrap of history" (16). In the age of the electronic media, therefore, an event has not entered history unless it is represented by that technology.

Here is an announcer who is calling what has become marked over the years as one of baseball's most "authentic" games, a game that over time has acquired an aura — which DeLillo's fiction unavoidably adds to even as it problematizes that aura. During the course of the game, Hodges recalls his years in Charlotte doing simulated broadcasts of Washington Senators' baseball games, "announcing" games he did not attend as the events came over the wire. His thoughts reveal that he, like DeLillo in *Underworld*,

liked to take the action into the stands, inventing a kid chasing a foul ball, a carrot-top boy with a cowlick (shameless, ain't I) who retrieves the ball and holds it aloft, this five-ounce sphere of cork, rubber, yarn, horsehide and spiral stitching, a souvenir baseball, a priceless thing somehow, a thing that seems to recapitulate the whole history of the game every time it is thrown or hit or touched. (26)

Hodges' recollections of simulated broadcasts, of course, call attention to the simulation DeLillo performs in calling up a long-ago game. The very fact that a recording of Hodges' broadcast exists is a fluke of mechanical reproduction, as DeLillo points out, because someone in Brooklyn decides to tape the game "and this will turn out to be the only known recording of Russ's famous account of the final moments of the game" (48). But the specificity of Hodges' remembering how he could create something out of the mere fact of a foul ball — figuring the winner of the scramble to recover the ball as the archetypal white boy — points to the way DeLillo challenges such mythologizing of baseball and America through his rendering of Cotter Martin's securing the ball Thomson hit.

Hodges, who thinks disparagingly of his simulated broadcasts in contrast to the glory of doing "real baseball" (25), misses a key point; namely, he still performs the same order of simulation in his broadcast of the game even when he is present because he still must flesh out all the details for his listeners if the game is to rise above the level of mere facts and statistics. Yet the mediation of radio, both for Hodges and his listeners, has become as invisible as an FBI wiretap. When a media form comes to seem transparent, when its role in the construction of aura is experienced paradoxically as an unmediated mediation, then we have entered, the novel suggests, the realm of the postmodern, technological sublime.

But if Hodges is, on the one hand, DeLillo's ironized self-figuration, he also points toward the political figure whose media career began by doing simulated broadcasts of baseball games — Ronald Reagan (Rogin, 11). Hodges's participation in the mythologizing of baseball parallels President Reagan's use of a mythological

American past. Whenever he waxed anecdotal, Reagan, as Michael Rogin points out, seemed either unable or unwilling to distinguish between Hollywood movies and American history (Rogin, 1–43). Reagan's conflation of film and history serves to embody a central contradiction of his presidency: despite the rhetoric of a classless society, the 1980s saw class differences sharpen. As the nostalgia president, Reagan attempted to return us to the prosperity of a mythologized, depoliticized 1950s, a 1950s that DeLillo in *Under-world* takes pains to show is altogether political and relevant to an understanding of the post-Cold War moment.

OF CONDOMOLOGY: AESTHETICIZING THE POLITICAL

Moving out from the prologue, it becomes clear that Hodges is only the first instance of the novel's reflexive figuration of the artist. *Underworld* is a novel peopled with a large number of artists and artist figures. Not only are there the literal and acknowledged artists—the painter Klara Sax and her friend Acey Greenwood, there are the underground artists whose work is often not granted the full status of art—the graffiti writer Ismael Muñoz and the satirical comic Lenny Bruce. But even this brief list only scratches the surface because there are a number of other characters that stand in for the artist. Through his secret files, J. Edgar Hoover himself, whose presentist interpretation of Bruegel's painting imagines nuclear apocalypse, figuratively becomes the auteur (he is, after all, the FBI's Director) of Cold War paranoia, transforming his personal pathology (his fear of germs that stand ready to invade the body) into a feature of American national identity. All of these characters allow DeLillo to think about the possibilities of aesthetic production. In short, through the repeated references to art and the large number of artist figures in the novel, DeLillo indirectly asks the question whether there is a oppositional function left to the artist in a postmodernity dominated by the electronic media and advertising. The American Marxist critic, Fredric Jameson, has suggested that multinational capital has now succeeded in appropriating the image to such an extent that all aesthetic production is nothing more than a form of commodity production. Against this totalizing sense of postmodernism, DeLillo retains some marginal hopes.

The titles of the various parts of *Underworld* signal DeLillo's interest in the issue of the image and its relation to the social. The direct references in the various section titles ask one to think simultaneously about the role and purpose of the image in high and mass culture. The prologue borrows the title of Bruegel's painting *The Triumph of Death*; Part 1, "Long Tall Sally," a Little Richard song; Part 3, "The Cloud of Unknowing," a fifth-century text of Catholic mysticism; Part 4, "Better Things for Better Living through Chemistry," an advertising slogan for Dow Chemical; Part 5, "Cocksucker Blues," the 1972 Robert Frank documentary film on the Rolling Stones; Part 6, "Arrangement in Gray and Black," the famous painting known popularly as "Whistler's Mother"; even the Epilogue, "Das Kapital," borrows the title of Karl Marx's famous critique of capitalism, a gesture that asks us to examine the function of the image in the political economy. The one title that seems to defy the pattern, that of Part 2, "Elegy for Left Hand Alone," actually works in the intersection of high and mass culture. Most immediately, the title refers to a moment when, sitting with his sister listening to a recording of a Saint-Saëns's piano work, Bronzini notices that "something dark seemed to enter, the soloist's left hand urging the tempo" (229); this something dark refers indirectly to the Texas Highway Killer, who in real life is a timid 42-year-old grocery checkout boy named Richard Gilkey who still lives at home, caring for his aging parents. To help disguise his identity, he teaches himself to shoot his victims "with the left hand"(266). Hence an

aesthetic experience is juxtaposed with the media celebrity of the
Texas Highway Killer, a point we will return to later.

While these titles insist on relating the aesthetic image to the
social, it becomes clear that not all images perform the same cultural work. There is in fact a continuum of aesthetic production
from images that are conceived and produced in full complicity
with capitalism to those images that attempt to gain a critical purchase on the political order. Du Pont's advertising slogan, of course,
is fully implicated, serving as a form of ideological waste management. The images implied by the slogan makes it difficult for
people to link the company with pollution. Yet with the vinyls, the
polymers, the plastics, and the pesticides come not just an increase
in immediate creature comforts (better things) but also the toxic
waste that means increased cancer rates and irrevocable damage to
the water table. Examined closely, the "better living" offered by
such chemical companies as Dow, one of the manufacturers of
Agent Orange, becomes a highly problematic image.

As we saw from DeLillo's representation of the baseball game,
the danger of turning politics into a matter of aesthetics is that it
dehistoricizes and turns the past into myth. DeLillo's rendering of
this early 1950s moment, then, is crucial to a scene that takes place
after the Cold War. In Chapter 5 of Part 2, Brian Glassic invites
Nick to the mall to see a new store with a striking name and focus —
Condomology. This boutique is devoted entirely to selling condoms
as instances of "better things." To these two men who came of age
in the 1950s, the entire ambiance of the store signals their memories of a time when there may have been a few brand names but all
condoms were more or less the same. From their simple role in the
1950s as a form of birth control and protection against treatable
venereal disease, the condoms of the 1990s are an index to postmodernity. In post-sexual revolution American, an age of HIV
and AIDS, the condom takes on a far different function that grants

the paranoia of the Cold War an afterlife in the sexuality of the present.

This store, a celebration to full-throttle libido, typifies the relation of multinational capital to consumer desire. The boutique stocks a seemingly endless proliferation of different varieties of condoms to fit the customer's sexual preferences: "finger condoms and full-body condoms, oral condoms with a minty flavor," condoms that are identified variously as "studded, snug, ribbed, bareback" (110). Reflecting on all the packaging involved in these products, Nick notes: "Behind the products and their uses we glimpsed the industry of vivid description. Dermasilk and astroglide and reservoir-tipped. There were condoms packaged as Roman coins and condoms in matchbox folders" (111). The "industry of vivid description," of course, is advertising and marketing.

But the store itself is a complete package, one that in large murals co-opts courtship images from the 1950s: "A boy and a girl in one of the murals sat in a booth with ice-cream sundaes and frosty glasses of water and long-handled spoons for the sundaes and the scene was not contrived to be charming but was close to documentary in tone and the whole place was a little museumlike . . ." (112). Overlaying the visual imagery, the almost subliminal tones of a 1950s crooner waft over the shopper. Clearly, Condomology doesn't just sell condoms; it sells lifestyles. As a marketing tool, the boutique sells its customers a sense of their sophistication, a sophistication knowable precisely against the innocence of a mythologized representation of the 1950s. If what the consumer experiences in Condomology is a sense of freedom, then it is an effect of capitalism's ability to conflate two fundamentally different notions of freedom: the Cold War, fought in the name of individual and political freedom, was in fact about free markets and consumer choice.

In a space that represents Jean Baudrillard's hyperreality writ large, the boundary between museum and store is blurred and the act of consumption is fully aestheticized. If capital today is more concerned with ensuring that individuals perform their social labor as consumers, then we can see Condomology as an instance of aestheticizing the political economy. In Walter Benjamin's terms, as I discussed earlier in Chapter 1, such an aestheticizing of the political is a defining feature of fascism. But in the age of the electronic media, it is a decentralized totalitarianism in which the nation state figures less and less.

Thus, Condomology is but a logical consequence of America's Cold War strategy. If America's Cold War policy was the containment of communism, then what must be contained in the post-Cold War period is the enormous amount of waste, both consumer and nuclear, that only grows exponentially as capitalism attempts to turn more of the world into conspicuous consumers. The winner of the Cold War was not America, but multinational capitalism, and 1950s America is just another image available to sell things. Yet capitalism faces a problem. If people become aware of the environmental threat of the waste of consumer society, there is a chance that a movement to consume less might emerge. Capital's solution is postmodern since it has less to do with the real than the modeling of the real: don't contain the growth of waste (since more waste means that business is good); rather, contain the appearance of waste.

What we might say is that DeLillo's novel, by using the condom as a motif, is itself a form of condomology, a study of waste and its containment. If capital through advertising is able to reify the shopping experience in consumer consciousness before the moment of purchase, what happens after the product has been used? This is precisely where DeLillo takes us in *Underworld* through Nick Shay's perspective. Nick works in the quintessential growth sector of the multinational economy — waste management.

Waste management, then, is closely related to aesthetics in *Underworld*. The older woman of Nick's affair in 1952 is Klara Sax, who after this episode leaves her husband and daughter in order to pursue art. She achieves fame in the 1960s through a pop art that constructs art out of the junk people have thrown away. In this way, Klara's and Nick's careers oddly reflect one another—both are waste managers. Nick's job, in essence, is to convince people that industrial and consumer waste does not exist by improving the technologies for the discreet removal of the visible traces of that waste. Like Nick, Klara makes invisible the waste of American culture, but with a twist. Klara's largest project, which is still ongoing in the novel's present, is a continuation of the recycling of junk that originally made her famous. Taking over an unused military base in the Arizona desert, Klara, along with a large group of volunteers under her direction, paints in rainbow colors the decommissioned B-52s that previously had carried the nuclear payload that could have annihilated humanity. With so vast a canvas, only an aerial view fully reveals the scope of this project—two hundred and thirty airplanes painted so far, the work continuing. Nick and his wife view this installation from a hot air balloon and sense the postmodern sublime:

> The piece had a great riverine wash, a broad arc of sage green or maybe mustard green with brushy gray disturbances, and it curved from the southeast corner up and across the north edge, touching nearly a third of the massed aircraft, several planes completely covered in the pigment—the work's circulating fluid, naming the pace, holding the surface together. (125)

Nick wonders "if the piece was visible from space like the land art of some lost Andean people" (126). Not merely hiding the detritus of America culture as Nick does (a thing surely dangerous to American's environmental awareness in and of itself), Klara in her waste management turns these B-52s into a site of aesthetic contemplation. Klara does have a political awareness; speaking to a reporter, she likens the post-Cold War moment to the end of WWII: "The one difference is we haven't actually fought a war this time. We have a number of postwar conditions without a war having been fought" (69–70). At the same time Klara emphasizes the aesthetic: "This is an art project, not a peace project" (70). Klara's art finally points to the implication of avant-garde art in the structures of high culture. This is not a people's art, since only a very few people have the economic means to view this massive installation. Still, her self-conscious attempt to create art out of waste is an incremental improvement over Hodge's mythologizing role that can turn trash (a used baseball) into a valuable commodity.

POLITICIZING THE AESTHETIC

If Russ Hodges and Klara Sax serve as DeLillo's reminder of the dangers of aestheticizing the political, then his other artist figures — Sergei Eisenstein, Lenny Bruce, and Ismael Muñoz — point us to various possibilities of politicizing the aesthetic. At nearly the structural mid-point of the novel, DeLillo turns to an explicitly political artist, the Russian filmmaker, Eisenstein, and his lost film, *Unterwelt*. While Eisenstein's art did get him in trouble with Soviet authorities in the 1930s, the film DeLillo describes is entirely his invention. No such film exists.

Unterwelt is doubly contextualized in the novel. Coming at the novel's midpoint, it mediates the apocalyptic and revelatory aesthetic images of the novel's prologue and epilogue — the Bruegel painting of the prologue and a billboard advertisement in the epilogue. But with Klara as our focalizer, *Unterwelt* is also sandwiched between two other films in Part 4. These other two postmodern films position Eisenstein's modernist art as an ideal for contemporary artists to aspire to.

As Klara attempts to get her artistic bearings in the summer of 1974, she attends screenings of three films—Robert Franks's disturbing documentary about the Rolling Stones on tour in America, *Cocksucker Blues* (which serves as the title of Part 4); the faux Eisenstein film; and an art film that endlessly loops multiple copies of the Zapruder film that captures the assassination of President Kennedy. All three say something explicit about waste.

The overt content of the first film, *Cocksucker Blues*, directly ties into the motif of waste in numerous ways. The behind the scenes glimpses of sex and drugs reveal an underside to the spotlight of the rock stage. Scenes of addicts shooting up with heroin, also known as smack (schmeck—shit—waste), flow into scenes of sex that border on rape. But more important than the wasteland implications of the film's content is how the film anticipates a trend of the 1980s and 90s. Here is a film about one of the most commercialized bands of the last third of the twentieth century. Franks' film may be ahead of the curve but nevertheless plays into what has become the infinite regress of the commodification of culture that is quintessentially postmodern: we don't just have the latest blockbuster film, but also the film about the making of the film; not just the rock tour, but the behind-the-scenes documentary about the tour.

A different film illustrates another aspect of postmodernity. Klara's lover Miles insists that she see an installation at a video artist's studio. Throughout the studio, there are multiple TV sets. The sets begin to show the shaky 8-millimeter home movie of the twenty seconds or so that capture Kennedy's death. The initial reaction of the audience is shock and horror, but with each iteration of the loop (some played in slow-motion, some at regular speed, each screen registering different frames), the viewers become increasingly more distanced. The shock wears off and the images become available for aesthetic contemplation. One stoned couple even starts making out. This art project may strive for creating fresh

perception, but it too says something about the postmodern condition. The Zapruder video installation finds its eerie double in the
novel in another piece of video, the film of the Texas Highway
Killer shooting a victim (Judson Rauch one of the owner's of the
Thomson baseball), an act accidentally captured by a girl with a
camcorder in another car. In an age where television news is just
another form of entertainment (and so another venue to sell products), once the media buys this film, it is shown repeatedly on TV
screens all over America, so much so that the viewer/consumer
experiences not the tragedy and pain of human suffering but a set
of slow-motion images stripped of all but formal aesthetic features.
What we see is how quickly what at first is an instance of avant-
garde art becomes the standard experience of any television viewer,
a kind of co-optation of aesthetic technique by capitalism.

Against the Frank film and the looping Zapruder film, DeLillo
centers a fantastic *Unterwelt*, the supposedly lost film recovered
from years of suppression in communist Europe and given a one-
time screening in Radio City Music Hall. In DeLillo's construction
of this non-existent silent film, his love for the medium and his
knowledge of Eisenstein are evident in his celebration of an artist
whose work can simultaneously evoke laughter and chilled awe:
"there was something to study in every frame, the camera place-
ment, the shapes and planes and the juxtaposed shots, the sense of
rhythmic contradiction, it was all spaces and volumes, it was tempo
mass and stress." In such filmmaking, "the camera angle is a kind
of dialectic" and scenes can be "extravagant, silly, of-kilter, and
technically impressive all at the same time" (429). Eisenstein's evocation of oppression in this science fiction nightmare vision leads
to Klara's speculations about the film as a political allegory. What is
perhaps more striking in the aftermath of the September 11, 2001
terrorist attack on the United States is how Klara's comments about
Eisenstein's filmic art seem to speak directly to the image that graces

the cover of *Underworld* by the modernist photographer André Kertész (1894–1985), who was born in Budapest but who moved to New York in 1936 where he remained for the rest of his life.

Troubling yet inarguably heavy-handed in its dialectic, the image, even when the novel appeared in 1997, seemed to fit too perfectly DeLillo's examination of the postmodern wasteland and the bleak possibilities of spiritual renewal in the age of multinational capital. With a foreboding play of light and shadow, Kertész's photograph suggests a dystopian metropolis. Centered and looming, though in the background, stand the twin towers of the World Trade Center. In the foreground appears a dark church. The cross on top of the church bisects the space between the two towers. But after the attack that killed nearly 5000 and reduced the WTC to a pile of rubble that has made it New York City's most pressing waste management project, the image chillingly reaches out to arrest one's attention further. Is that large object a plane that appears to be flying dangerously close to, seemingly heading toward, one of the towers? No, it's a large bird. The upper floors of the towers just above the bird are obscured by a thick fog that all too disturbingly resembles the smokechoked skies of New York on that September morning after the airliners had crashed into the towers. The image pushes us toward a sense of the uncanny, a sense that is only further heightened by the story of how the image came to be used as the cover for *Underworld*. DeLillo himself found the photograph but was worried that it might be too religious. His editor at Scribner, Nan Graham, then hired a photo researcher to find a cover image: "she came back with the same image DeLillo had found on his own" (Passaro, "Don DeLillo and the Towers"). Both the image and the story behind the image work to produce an eerie, doubled, and contradictory response toward *Underworld*'s cover; simultaneous beliefs that it cannot possibly and surely must be prophetic shimmer within the same photo. It is our new uncanny relation to Kertész's art that helps us understand DeLillo's apparent identification with outsider artists such as Eisenstein and Ismael Muñoz whose work inspires awe.

Despite DeLillo's obvious preference of Eisenstein's art over that of the other two films of Part 4, the power of Eisenstein's art has been contained both by the commodified conditions of its screening (the Rockettes perform a high-kicking routine in military garb as the prelude to the screening) and the film's own high modernist technical pretension. During the intermission of the film, however (which occurs near the structural and temporal midpoint of the novel), Klara notices the presence of a different underworld, the rumbling of a subway train passing under the theater.

The subway cars that pass beneath the theater are covered with the work of another artist figure, Ismael Muñoz, who most fully represents the possibility of politicizing the aesthetic. Known as Moonman 157 in the 1970s, he is famous in the underground world of New York graffiti artists for his distinctive designs on subway cars. Against Klara, who is an insider in the world of New York art circles, Ismael maintains his outsider status throughout his career, despite attempts of the art world to find him for a showing of his work when graffiti art was in vogue in the 1970s. His very name, which suggests simultaneously the biblical and Herman Melville's Ishmael, confirms the marginality he embodies through his class, race, and bisexuality.

Before considering the artist Ismael becomes in the post-Cold War period, it is important to consider DeLillo's figuration of Lenny Bruce and his jazz aesthetic. Each section has an artist figure that either narrates or focalizes the reader's perceptions. In Part 5, Bruce serves this function as we following him from West Hollywood to New York City during the Cuban Missile Crisis in the week of October 22, 1962. Bruce's satiric improvisations, which use the possibility of nuclear annihilation to rend all middle-class and counter-cultural pretense, are crystallized in the repeated line he mockingly howls in city after city: "We're all gonna die!" Bruce is the fragmented, postexistentialist who seems at times more controlled by than controlling the many cultural voices that he channels, a precursor if you will for those who claim that the affect of our millennial moment is something closer now to schizophrenia than paranoia: "All the Lennies. The persecuted junkie. The antihypocrite. The satirist and nose picker. Lenny the hipster fink. Lenny the ass mechanic, girl-spotting in hotel lobbies. Lenny the vengeance of the Lord." (507). His fragmented identities produce an equally fragmented art:

He did psychoanalysis, personal reminiscence, he did voices and accents, grandmotherly groans, scenes from prison movies, and he finally closed the show with a monologue that had a kind of abridged syntax, a thing without connectives, he was cooking free-form, closer to music than speech, doing a spoken jazz in which a slang term generates a matching argot, like musicians trading fours, the road band, the sideman's inner riff, and when the crowd dispersed they took this rap mosaic with them into the strip joints and bars and late-night diners . . . and it was Lenny's own hard bop, his speeches to the people that rode the broad Chicago night. (586)

Bruce's jazz-like improvisational riffs on American culture reflect DeLillo's own aesthetic practice in "Better Things for Better Living Through Chemistry." The fragmented structure of Part 5 mimics a Bruce monologue with its abrupt shifts in context. As in Bruce's performance, DeLillo's art aspires to the condition of linguistic jazz.

But despite an apparent identification with Bruce, DeLillo does not sentimentalize the heroin-addicted comic, who remains "showbiz." Bruce is not about a political agenda and he satirizes beatnik counterculture as well as the middle class. What DeLillo celebrates, though, is Bruce's ability to touch his audience in a direct and profound way, so that his voice is "the idlike wail from [the audi-ence's] own souls, the desperate buried place where you demand recognition of primitive rights and need" (547). For a writer such as DeLillo who has so openly wondered whether there is any cul-tural work left for the novel and the novelist in the age of the electronic media, the ability of Bruce's art to create affect expresses DeLillo's hope for his own aesthetic practice.

The final section in which Lenny appears is the show that culminates his hectic week of touring. However, on this night, October 29, 1963, the missile crisis has passed and the immediate prospect for apocalypse has receded. Before a crowd of 3000 at Carnegie Hall, Lenny becomes tired of his old material and strives for something more. He pays homage to a paranoid black street preacher, who Lenny happens to hear late one night in Harlem. (This is the same preacher that Manx Martin stops to listen to the night he sells the Thomson home run ball.) But as Bruce does so, he falls into the voice of the old African-American man, whose paranoid rhapsodies on the dollar bill as the symbolic key to the apocalypse have a strange power. The audience feels uncomfortable because they're not sure if Bruce is making fun of the old man and more uncomfortable still "because he could not seem to stop doing the voice. It was as if the voice had been crossed with his. It was as if cross-voices were unavoidable, whether you knew it or not, whether you liked it or not, and maybe this old black man spoke in Lenny's voice at times, alone, unknowing, in his room . . ." (628). Lenny knows the street preacher saw him but also knows that the old man's audience is the small crowd of dispossessed, the "wastelings of the lost world, the lost country that exists right here in America." From this moment, Bruce begins to improvise a bit about a virgin living in a whorehouse who blows smoke rings from her vagina and is saved from a life of degradation by an eccentric millionaire who falls in love with her. This bit of Bruce's sick sexual humor, however, implodes as the comic loses interest in the punchline before he delivers it. Bruce suddenly starts dismantling the narrative, questioning its logic, admitting that the millionaire was made up, that the girl wasn't from San Juan, and that there were never any smoke rings. Destroying his audience's mood, Bruce returns to the story, this time "to tell the truth":

> You take the subway to the South Bronx, where she lives with her junkie mother who can't kick. She's barely old enough so that men are beginning to notice. Her mother comes and goes. . . . Landlord's been coming around. Or putting dispossesses under the door because you never actually see him. He's a corporation called XYZ Realty with a post office box in Greenland. The girl's hiding in the empty lots, down the maze of back alleys, because her mother's gone again and she thinks the landlord will have her arrested. Let's make her human. Let's give her a name."
>
> But he didn't give her a name. (632–33)

Bruce doesn't give her a name because he can't, but DeLillo can and has. A central episode in the epilogue to *Underworld* is the rape and murder of Esmeralda Lopez, a homeless girl living in the South Bronx whose death is memorialized by Ismael Muñoz.

In Bruce's culminating monologue, then, we have the representation of the possibilities of art to exceed the intentions of the artist, so much so that the artist may become prophetic in ways beyond his or her comprehension. In his identification with the old African-American street preacher, Bruce momentarily stops being simply an entertainer in order to address the same audience of dispossessed that are the street preacher's audience; moreover, Lenny seems to have been granted access to the miraculous — what Pynchon's Jesús Arrabal, the anarchist in *The Crying of Lot 49*, might term an anarchist miracle — "another world's intrusion into this one" (120).

Defying all narrative logic, Bruce begins to tell the story of a doomed girl not yet born. It will take DeLillo's supreme underground artist, Ismael, to finish the tale.

Ismael is another waste manager whose art is linked to a jazz aesthetic. In this regard, Ismael emerges as the underground version of Klara Sax. The origin of Ismael's art is literally found underground in the subway tunnels he walked as a teenager. There he discovers both the pleasures of homosexual encounters and a bit of graffiti scrawled on one of the subterranean wall: "*Bird Lives*" (435). He only later discovers that this is a reference to the legendary jazz tenor saxophonist, Charlie Parker. But learning of the referent, Ismael chooses Parker as one of his precursors. Klara, after her divorce from Bronzini, returns to her maiden name, but with a twist, refashioning "Sachs" into "Sax," which is Parker's instrument. Ismael's art becomes a central focus of *Underworld*'s "Das Kapital" epilogue. That is because of the role he sees for his public deployment of the image. Even in his days as Moonman 157, Ismael had a sense of a mission to his painting (or "tagging") subway cars, which he articulates as an aesthetic (one echoing the rats' alleys of Eliot's *Waste Land*): "The trains come roaring down the rat alleys all alike and then you hit a train and it is yours, seen everywhere in the system, and you get inside people's heads and vandalize their eyeballs" (435). Defacing public property is not the point of his graffiti; creating fresh perspective for his viewers is.

Like Klara, Ismael in the post-Cold War moment has an ongoing installation known as The Wall, which he and his crew use to commemorate the deaths of underclass children in New York. Klara's installation is located in a literal wasteland, the desert, while Ismael's stands in the urban wasteland, a part of the Bronx so blighted that a tour bus, South Bronx Surreal, brings in groups of foreigners who photograph the sights. The inspiration for Klara's

installation, as Mark Osteen has discussed (254–55) is Sabato Rodia's Watts Towers, which she visits while in Los Angeles in 1974
and which helps to bring end her artist's block. From 1921 to1955
Rodia, an immigrant untrained in architecture or engineering, con-
structed elaborate and fantastic steel-frame towers over 100 feet tall,
largely from the waste of consumer culture — soda, beer, and wine
bottles, fragments of mirrors and tiles — mixed together with cement,
pebbles, and shells. Here is an art that manages waste in an anti-
representational fashion, refusing to invest commodities with desire
and instead constructing a personal vision out of the remains of
consumer culture. But while Klara may experience an epiphany in
her encounter with Rodia's art and be able to reproduce in her
desert installation the playfulness of Watts Towers, Ismael, although
he has never seen the Towers, appears to be the truer descendant
of Rodia. Unlike Klara's remote and inaccessible art, Ismael's (like
Rodia's) is part of the urban landscape. When a particularly violent
death occurs, the rape and murder of homeless girl, Esmeralda
Lopez, Ismael's Wall is given "two and a half seconds" of CNN
coverage" (816) as part of the media attention to this crime. What
makes the news coverage particularly eerie is that Ismael and his
crew see the moment on their television, which is powered by a
generator that is itself powered one of Ismael's crew members ped-
aling a bicycle:

They gawk and buzz, charged with a kind of second sight, the things they
know so well seen inside out, made new and nationwide. They stand there
smeared in other people's seeing. Then the anchorwoman comes on. They
tell Willamette to pedal faster man because the picture is beginning to fade
and the anchorwoman's electric red hair is color-running from her head in
a luminous ring, which makes her all the more amazing, and she describes
their lives to them in a bell-tone virgin voice, a woman so striking of feature
she makes the news her own. . . . (816–17)

This moment, functioning again in Baudrillard's hyperreal, shows the ability of mass media to construct a powerful imagistic aura, one that seems to draw its power by draining the energy from other images, such as Ismael's political art. The woman newscaster is the same one who interviewed the Texas Highway Killer when he called in during her broadcast to discuss his crimes. This link shows how the imagistic space of network news airs events on the basis of their entertainment value. The image burn of Ismael's Wall is less than three seconds (much less important then than the ramblings of a madman/media star such as the Texas Highway Killer), but even in this brief instant, the Wall has been reduced to a visual commodity.

At this point in the epilogue, DeLillo turns to an aesthetic image apparently linked to the supernatural and a revelation, an image that might counter the false aura of the television broadcast. Crowds begin to gather each evening to witness a billboard where an image of the murdered child appears briefly whenever a subway train illuminates the back of the billboard. It is in this moment that DeLillo's homage to Thomas Pynchon's *The Crying of Lot 49* becomes clearest. Waste has been a dominant motif in *Underworld*, and the very word resonates with Pynchon's pairing of waste with the possibility of revelation, for in *Lot 49* waste is also an acronym (We Await Silent Tristero's Empire) of the dispossessed who use a centuries old underground postal system to communicate. In *Underworld*, DeLillo's dispossessed await the train that apparently brings them the revelation that Pynchon's characters so desire.

But Pynchon's novel is not the only intertext in play at this moment. A fuller appreciation of what is at stake in the epilogue's billboard scene is available if one reads it against Fitzgerald's own underworld novel about the distinctions of social class in New York City, *The Great Gatsby* (1925). In DeLillo's novel, Nick Shay (whose name of course reminds us he is Irish as well as Italian) always wonders if the criminal underworld killed his father, while Fitzgerald's Nick Carraway feels the taint of the underworld by his association with Jay Gatsby, who brings Nick into contact with Meyer Wolfsheim, "who fixed the World Series back in 1919" (74). The opening of Chapter 2 of *Gatsby* identifies a section of urban blight that train commuters saw crossing the Queensborough bridge from Long Island to New York as the "valley of ashes" and (in an obvious nod to T.S. Eliot's famous poem about the spiritual degradation of modernity) "the waste land" (23–24). Fitzgerald's impressionistic valley of ashes was in reality the Corona dumps, a large swampy area (now the site of the New York Met's Shea Stadium). In the 1920s, this dump was being filled with ashes from coal-burning furnaces—as well as with horse manure and garbage. As DeLillo's Nick would surely recognize, Fitzgerald is describing a site of waste management.

Like Fitzgerald's billboard, DeLillo's is also placed in a wasteland where there are "tall weeds and the waste burner coughing toxic fumes and the old railroad bridge spanning the Harlem River." There stands "an advertising sign scaffolded high above the riverbank and meant to attract the doped-over glances of commuters on the trains that run incessantly down from the northern suburbs into the thick of Manhattan money and glut" (818). In *Gatsby*, the billboard advertising an optometrist, with its representation of gigantic eyes looking out of a pair of enormous glasses, comes to suggest the absence of any transcendent moral perspective when George Wilson, deranged after his wife's death, equates the unblinking eyes of Dr. T. J. Eckleburg with God because both see everything. But DeLillo refigures Wilson's deranged conflation of the billboard with a supernatural presence by making the spiritual possibility of *Underworld*'s billboard a crowd's collective experience. And clearly the epilogue's crowd at the billboard directs us back to the prologue's crowd at the baseball game.

If *Underworld* represents the fragments DeLillo has shored against Nick's ruin, it is symbolically appropriate that J. Edgar Hoover's double, Sister Edgar (Nick's childhood teacher) should be our angle of vision of the billboard. If J. Edgar mediates in the prologue on Bruegel's *The Triumph of Death*, Sister Edgar provides in the epilogue a knowing perspective on the imagery represented by the advertisement:

A vast cascade of orange juice pouring diagonally from the top right into a goblet that is handheld at lower left—the perfectly formed hand of a female caucasian of the middle suburbs. Distant willows and vaguish lake view set the social locus. But it is the juice that commands the eye, thick and pulpy with a ruddled flush that matches the madder moon. And the first detailed drops splashing at the bottom of the goblet with a scatter of spindrift, each fleck embellished with the finicky rigor of some precisionist painting. What a lavishment of effort and technique, no refinement spared—the equivalent, Edgar thinks, of medieval church architecture. And the six-ounce cans of Minute Maid arrayed across the bottom of the board, a hundred identical cans so familiar in design and color and typeface that they have personality, the convivial cuteness of little orange-and-black people. (820)

Rather than the triumph of death, capitalism, in the form of advertising, celebrates the triumph of consumption, which is the denial of death. (Thirty years earlier, the Madison Avenue executive Charles Wainwright, third owner of the Thomson baseball, had envisioned an orange juice campaign strikingly similar to the one Edgar views.) That this billboard is erected in an area of urban poverty underscores the ideological function of advertising that represents the middle class as the unquestioned norm.

Over and above the issue of technique and advertising's appropriation of the category of public art, the implications that reside in the gorgeous image of orange juice are highly freighted in the novel's symbolic logic and suggest waste in many forms. While serving in Vietnam, Nick's brother, Matt, notices the black drums at the edge of the camp and learns that planes were

spraying the jungles with a herbicide stored in black drums that had identifying orange stripes. . . .
The drums resembled cans of frozen Minute Maid enlarged by a crazed strain of DNA. And the substance in the drums contained, so the rumor went, a cancer-causing agent. (463)

Reflecting on his war experience in the summer of 1974, Matt reiterates the link between the image of orange juice and waste when he wonders "how can you tell the difference between orange juice and agent orange if the same massive [distribution] system connects them at levels outside your comprehension?" (465). Returning to DeLillo's description of the Minute Maid billboard, it is possible to see the racial underside of the image. Against the white hand that is a metonymy for the white middle class is the crowd of "little orange-and-black people" that the cans suggest. These little people are simultaneously the Vietnamese victims of agent orange and people of color in the United States who fall outside the parameters of middle-class consumption. More broadly, if agent orange was a weapon used in a local "hot" war during the Cold War, then orange juice — as a site of capitalism's appropriation of the aesthetic image to construct an American identity that transforms political freedom into freedom of consumer choice — was surely part of America's Cold War effort.

Despite Sister Edgar's conviction that the source of the revelation is God, the novel strongly implies that Ismael is responsible for the image of Esmeralda appearing in the billboard's orange juice advertisement. That the image depends on the headlights of a subway train points to the fact that Ismael's first art was marking subway cars. When Sister Edgar arrives to witness the miracle, she notices

Ismael and his crew in attendance. In his earlier avatar as Moon-man, Ismael liked to be in the crowds at the subway stations to see the responses of people to his art. Perhaps most tellingly, the punishment for those caught marking cars in the 1970s, as Ismael knows, had been to wash those cars in orange juice, since the acid in the juice dissolved the paint. In this regard, Ismael stands to Charles Wainwright as Cotter Martin stands to Bill Waterson. In the prologue's 1950s American race relations were themselves contained in a kind of master Us-Them binary of white and black. After the baseball game, Cotter forces Bill to see the world anew when the African-American youth appropriates the ball. But in the multiracial 1990s, the Hispanic Ismael challenges and subverts Wainwright's desire to construct the perceiving subject as Anglo-Saxon.

When the first train approaches Sister Edgar experiences the revelation felt by the crowd, hearing the "holler of unstoppered belief" and sees "a dozen women clutch their heads, they whoop and sob, a spirit, a godsbreath passing through the crowd" (821). Eight minutes later with the next train's arrival, Edgar

sees Esmeralda's face take shape under the rainbow of bounteous juice and above the little suburban lake and there is a sense of someone living in the image, an animating spirit—less than a tender second of life, less than half a second and the spot is dark again. (822)

Here it seems is a subversion of advertising's colonization of the aesthetic. Ismael's discovery of a new aesthetic technique that simultaneously subverts specious aura while producing authentic aura suggests that there is still a role for an outsider art that stays a half-step ahead of advertising's near total control of the image by multinational capital. But just a half-step. In a few days the crowds begin to spiral out of control and threaten social order. When the crowds return one night, they see only a blank billboard advertising itself as *"Space Available"* (824).

DeLillo seems to use the novel's various artist figures to think about his own position as a novelist. Aware that his own vast fictional canvas (*Underworld*, after all, is 827 pages) may render his art as remote from contemporary cognizance as Klara's desert installation, DeLillo earlier, as I pointed out in the backgrounds section, has addressed in *Mao II* his concern that the novelist's role in culture has been usurped by the terrorist. The figure of Ismael, the outsider artist whose work assaults the viewer, represents the terrain of cognitive vandalism within which DeLillo wishes to work. Although the final word of the novel is "Peace," *Underworld* is not a peace project; it is an attempt to construct fully historicized art.

The epilogue's exploration of the possibility of authentic aesthetic aura makes the conclusion of the novel's prologue deeply ironic. Near the end of the prologue, the game is over, but many fans remain in the stands and on the field. Russ has finished his interviews in the locker rooms and is preparing to leave when his producer, Al, remarks:

> "Mark the spot. Like where Lee surrendered to Grant or some such thing."
>
> Russ thinks this is another kind of history. He thinks they will carry something out of here that joins them all in a rare way, that binds them to a memory with protective power. . . . Isn't it possible that this midcentury moment enters the skin more lastingly than the vast shaping strategies of eminent leaders, generals steely in their sunglasses—the mapped visions that pierce our dreams? Russ wants to believe a thing like this keeps us safe in some undetermined way. (59–60)

What DeLillo's Hodges describes here is what Benjamin identifies as aura. The sense of a protective power Hodges experiences is what is pernicious in Benjamin's view, for the false aura of sport masks not only the politics of Cold War America but also the most fundamental reality of life, personal mortality. Hodges reflections continue:

This is the thing that will pulse in his brain come old age and double vision and dizzy spells—the surge sensation, the leap of people already standing, that bolt of noise and joy when the ball went in. This is the people's history and it has flesh and breath that quicken to the force of this old safe game of ours. And fans at the Polo Grounds today will be able to tell their grandchildren—they'll be the gassy old men leaning into the next century and trying to convince anyone willing to listen, pressing in with medicine breath, that they were here when it happened. (60)

The veneration of origin and celebration of athletic genius serves to displace personal mortality, recontextualizing it in the space of a timeless tradition. To the extent that the Dodgers-Giants game has an immortal life, the fans who witnessed the game participate in that immortality; if one is present at the constructive moment of aura—or so this quasi-religious logic runs—then one is always part of that aura.

Benjamin's sense that mechanical reproduction could be used to construct aura in mass culture that would aestheticize the political has become in DeLillo's contemporary America more pervasive than Benjamin ever could have imagined. It matters not whether one seeks escape into a timeless tradition by contemplating the relation between the 1951 Dodgers-Giants' playoff series and the 2000 Mets-Yankees' World Series or by meditating on the relative value of metaphysical versus Romantic poetry. The point here is something more than that baseball in its quasi-religious function is the opiate of the American masses. In the mass media's reflection of the masses back to themselves, there is a structuring of subjectivity conducive to an ahistorical formalist contemplation of the media forms themselves. When people seek a surrender to a transcendent power, the Führer figure will always appear to emerge, if only as pure media construct.

Seen from a more fully historicized perspective, the final image of *Underworld*'s prologue serves as an apt figuration of America reality after 1951. A drunk on the field, participating in the postgame celebration begins to run the bases; as he approaches second, Hodges and his friend "see that he is going to slide and they stop and watch him leave his feet" (60). For his watchers, "all the fragments of the afternoon collect around his airborne form. Shouts, bat-cracks, full bladders, and stray yawns, the sand-grained manyness of things that can't be counted" (60). The fragments that can't be counted include Cold War politics and race-class difference. Postwar America, with its exaggerated sense of exceptionalism, is the suspended drunk of the postgame celebration, the text suggests. The drunk is frozen in the last moment of euphoria over American long-ball power, our exclusive possession of the big blast.

WASTE MANAGEMENT IN THE NEW WORLD ORDER

A different portion of the novel's epilogue, "Das Kapital," balances the prologue by bringing the reader full circle as one travels to an old nuclear test site in Kazakhstan. A Russian entrepreneur has brought Nick to the exact spot of the October 3, 1951 atomic blast that had made the Soviet Union a superpower. Nick is there to witness a test for the potential commercial use of underground nuclear explosions — the elimination of hazardous wastes (including nuclear waste) from first-world countries. The losers of the Cold

War will "clean up" by literally cleaning up for the winners. This visit to post-Cold War Russia is chilling for two reasons. First, DeLillo shows the way Russian culture is attempting to ape the worst of Western consumerism. In a Russian bar called the Football Hooligan, where paid doubles of Lenin, Marx, and Trotsky mix with the crowd, Nick senses the force of multinational capital:

Foreign investment, global markets, corporate acquisitions, the flow of information through transactional media, the attenuating influence of money that's electronic and sex that's cyberspaced, untouched money and computer safe sex, the convergence of consumer desire—not that people want the same things, necessarily, but that they want the same range of choices. (785)

The bar represents Fredric Jameson's postmodern, a space wherein previously articulated styles blur in a dizzying confusion that erases the specificity of time and place. Relating the epilogue's opening to the novel's overall concern with waste, aesthetics, and history, one can see that DeLillo constitutes himself as a waste manager, since his project has been to scavenge and recover what, to borrow Marx's metaphor, has been relegated to the trash heap of history.

The second and more disturbing view of the former Soviet Union is Nick's visit to a local clinic for the unacknowledged and in some instances grotesquely disfigured victims of nuclear testing. The victimization is not limited to a single generation, since genetic mutations have increased the cancer rates of this population's children and grandchildren. Here is waste that cannot be managed, and we are reminded that these people are as much war casualties as were those killed in any of the local "hot" wars (Vietnam, Afghanistan) during the period of US-Soviet rivalry.

In his eleventh novel, DeLillo urges Americans to acknowledge the cost, both in personal identity and world resources, of our Cold

War "victory." He further suggests that, although the threat of nuclear holocaust may have receded, a secular apocalypse may be at
hand if multinational corporations do succeed in turning the entire
world into a homogenous consumer culture. In our accelerating
rate of consumption, we are producing the underworld of literal
waste or garbage that will consume us. America may have "won"
the Cold War but at what price? From individual families buying
fallout shelters in the 1950s to Reagan's "Star Wars" Strategic Defense Initiative in the 1980s, much of America's real and symbolic
capital was spent in the maintenance of a definition, an ability to
distinguish ourselves from our Cold War Other, the Soviet Union.
The demise of Reagan's Evil Empire and the end of the Cold War
means that this master Us-Them binary of the 1950s through the
early 1990s can no longer mask the effects of multinational capital
in a period of increasing globalization. And certainly no mythologized history of our great American pastime can contain identity as
the United States becomes increasingly racially diverse. *Underworld*
may not ensure the production of a "solid historiographic formation
on the reader's part" (*Postmodernism*, 24) that Fredric Jameson
requires before he will grant any political vocation to contemporary
historical fiction (and perhaps one may wonder why any cultural
text should have to shoulder such a burden alone); however, *Underworld* opens a site wherein historical thinking becomes possible.
And in so doing, DeLillo makes a case that some cultural work
remains for the novel as a genre.

CODA: EXITING THE WASTELAND

Although the main action of *Underworld* ends in 1992, the novel
takes us much nearer the present in its final pages. The now semi-
retired Nick, along with the reader, surfs the web, starting at a site

his son, Jeff, discovers: *http://blk.www/dd.com/miaculum* (810). This moment adds a bit of metafictionality inasmuch as one of DeLillo's characters visits a fictitious web site created by "dd" of the web address. But more important than the metafictionality is what these scenes of web surfing say about contemporary identity. Against Nick's final moment of first-person narration in which he expresses his longing for a lost authentic identity in which he was "dumbmuscled and angry and real" (810), the novel seems to shift to a third-person omniscience once the reader is on the other side of the web address. Yet the "omniscience" is filtered through Nick, who is looking at the screen for us. Here we learn of Esmeralda's and Sister Edgar's deaths. And in Edgar's death she ends up not in heaven but in cyberspace, linked to her double, J. Edgar Hoover. Still, Nick's presence in the final pages emerges despite the apparent omniscience of the narrative voice through the repeated direct addresses to the implicated reader. And we are left with a postmodern question to ponder: "Is cyberspace a thing within the world or is it the other way around? Which contains the other, and how can you tell for sure?" (826). That is, does the web model the real or has this hyperreality become the Real?

In terms of individual identity, the implications of DeLillo's cyberspace, however, seem less than fully liberating, certainly not a celebration of the free play of an empowered computer user. If *Underworld* has shown us characters who are trying to make connections in order to interpret the world (as Matt Shay does when he sees the connection between Agent Orange and orange juice in capital's systems of distribution), the novel ends in the place where everything is indeed connected. But the connections of the web do not seem conducive to the construction of a resisting subjectivity that might attain some critical purchase on capitalism. Rather, with ever-increasing stores of information available and hyperlinked (as often as not to a virtual checkout counter and the commercial opportunity to buy something), the possibility of individual interpretation — however paranoid it might be — implodes into the schizophrenic flow of information. In other words, the connections of the web already outstrip the fantasies of the most dedicated paranoid.

Much as Eliot's *Waste Land* closes with a benediction ("Shantih shantih shantih," which Eliot explains in his notes to his poem as the Hindu equivalent of "The peace which passeth understanding"), *Underworld* concludes with a meditation on the etymology of the novel's final word, "Peace" (827). What we might say is that the novel concludes with a call to readers to do what DeLillo's novel suggests may be impossible, namely, to hang on to their paranoia because paranoia creates the possibility of resistance to the total flow of capital. But happily for us, DeLillo models this behavior by his (possibly paranoid) reading of cyberspace.

3

The Novel's Reception

DeLillo's eleventh novel was published officially on October 3, 1997 in the United States (the forty-sixth anniversary of the third and deciding playoff game between the Dodgers and the Giants for the 1951 National League pennant). British publication by Picador followed in January 1998. A long-anticipated publication event, *Underworld* was widely reviewed by the print media. By and large, the initial reviews in both the United States and United Kingdom were highly laudatory. But whether positive or critical, because of the nature of reviews (reviewers often work with strict word limits), many of the observations tend toward the impressionistic.

A sample of some of the briefer positive reviews yields these characterizations of *Underworld*. In a Boston *Globe* review, Gail Caldwell writes: "DeLillo has dared something in this novel outside the reach of most contemporary fiction, which is to map the last half-century of America's forward march, flood that terrain with personal tragedies and cultural analysis and the cruel coincidences of passion, then bring his story home again." Eileen Battesby notes in *The Irish Times* that "*Underworld* is to the end of the American literary century what John Dos Passos's U.S.A. trilogy was to its early decades" and concludes with this praise: "Stylish, humane, daring, this dazzling performance possesses wisdom, and integrity to match its awesome technique, style and scale." Writing for the London *Telegraph*, Christopher Bigsby calls *Underworld* an instance of "the Great American Novel" and expands Battesby's American genealogy of the novel, calling it the result of "Walt Whitman, Theodore Dreiser, John Dos Passos and Thomas Pynchon meeting in a vacant car lot in the Bronx to compare notes." Another reviewer who identifies *Underworld* as the "great American novel" is David Wiegand. Writing in the *San Francisco Chronicle*, Wiegand praises DeLillo's "millennial hypothesis: that a civilization is defined and destroyed, not (as prevailing theory has it) by what it creates but by what it throws away — from household trash and atomic waste to human values and lives." Andrew Pyper in the *Montreal Gazette* also invokes "the Great American Novel" label to praise DeLillo's "dead-on characterizations," "his original, funny and utterly precise prose style," and the novel's "rare technical mastery." Lauding *Underworld*'s "towering ambition" and "immense formal complexity," Philip Marchand in the *Toronto Star* claims that "DeLillo's novel represents the most urgent, far-reaching attempt in recent American fiction to wake us up from our collective sleepwalk through the '90s."

Several reviewers noted that *Underworld* represents DeLillo's maturation in his portrayal of character. Michiko Kakutani in her *New York Times* review says that while readers will find all the themes they are familiar with from DeLillo's previous novels, *Underworld* represents a positive development. For Kakutani if DeLillo's previous novels were "shrewd and absurdly comic" they were "also a little chilly and sociological in effect"; but in *Underworld* there is "a new sympathy and attention to character" that makes it "DeLillo's most affecting novel yet." British novelist Martin Amis, writing in the *New York Times Book Review*, senses that DeLillo's treatment of character may be quite personal since the normally remote DeLillo seems more present in *Underworld*: "It has an undertow of personal pain, having to do with fateful irreversibilities in a young life—a register that DeLillo has never touched before."

Although praising DeLillo's delineation of character, Luc Sante and Michael Wood, writing in the *New York Review of Books* and the *London Review of Books* respectively, cast matters somewhat differently than Kakutani and Amis. Sante and Wood feel that DeLillo is not just creating rounded characters and that the effect of these characters' voices is not entirely realistic. Speaking of the many minor characters, Sante notes that "DeLillo balances the characters' perfectly observed idiomatic speech with his own laconic rough-edged brushstroke of a voice, and when he is attributing thoughts to those characters manages somehow to frame them in a style that glides between their voices and his." Wood takes this point a bit further claiming that DeLillo's characters "talk like people who are weirdly able to discuss and picture their lives as they live them, whose intelligence never sleeps and doesn't pause for realism" and that "they talk and think the way everyone would if they had a writer lurking in their consciousness."

For both Blake Morrison and Andrew O'Hagan, *Underworld* epitomizes the achievement of American fiction, an achievement that calls into question the efforts of contemporary British novelists. Writing in the *London Independent*, Morrison says that reading *Underworld* "prompts the thought that even the most talented and ambitious of British novelists find it hard to work on this size canvas, at any rate when they're writing about Britain." O'Hagan's *VLS* review goes even further. Noting the decline of British prose fiction, O'Hagan asserts that the best stylists of the English language are now from India, Ireland, Scotland, and the United States and goes on to ask "Where is the English novelist with the imaginative gumption to enter, subcutaneously, as DeLillo does, into the world of supermarkets, all-night gas stations, denatured submarine bases, hinterland housing projects, food-processing plants, the secret history of the soil beneath you, and the whole underworld of public and private affairs, all wired from the breathing perspective of the new family."

Despite the strong chorus of reviewers (far more than I could cite here) hailing *Underworld* as the latest instance of the Great American Novel, there were a few naysayers. Michael Dibdin in his *Sunday London Times* review admits that "the evocations of life in the Italian community of the Bronx in the 1950s" are "wonderfully fresh and compelling" and that DeLillo is a "virtuoso at 'bits' and jazzy riffs" but feels that the bits fail to "add up to more than the sum or their parts." More problematic for Dibdin, "the lengthy extrapolations of the subject of waste . . . ultimately overwhelm the fictional fabric of the book very much like waste itself, through sheer quantity." John Leonard, in a flippant review that appears in *The Nation* seems more intent on demonstrating his wit than in engaging the complexity of the novel. Claiming that DeLillo, "the posterboy for postmodernism," reveals himself to be "a secret Holy Roller," Leonard gleefully ceases on DeLillo's apparent representation of spiritual possibility in order to take literature professors to task for having been foolish enough to read the author in the context of postmodern theory. Given the novel's ending, in which crowds believe they have experienced a "redemptive act of grace," Leonard believes that DeLillo's entire fictional career is not a reading of postmodernity but nothing more than an attempt to "see through signs to the sacred." For Leonard, the novel's ending renders *Underworld* "gratuitous." (My reading of the billboard in the preceding chapter, I hope, suggests something quite the opposite.) Harsher still, Leonard sees DeLillo's representation of paranoia as indistinguishable from the author's own paranoid fantasies: "Always seeking value, he is preternaturally alert to its absence or corruption," which makes *Underworld* (and by implication DeLillo) "*unbalanced.*"

Unquestionably, though, the longest and most engaged negative review is James Woods's "Black Noise" in *The New Republic*. For Woods, "*Underworld* proves, once and for all, or so I must hope, the incompatibility of paranoid history with great fiction." The representation of political paranoia for Woods's poetics is "bad for the novel" as a genre "because it is a mysticism facing a form that exists to repel it. Paranoia has an unlicensed freedom that outraces fiction, whose formal task is to establish a licensed freedom." If one follows Woods's position, however, it is difficult to imagine how a novelist might write about an age that by its very master Us-Them binary (United States vs. Soviet Union) engendered political paranoia from the Cuban Missile Crisis, to Watergate, to Ronald Reagan's Star Wars missile defense initiative to combat the Evil Empire. Woods turns to DeLillo's essay "The Power of History" to argue that the novelist has become a later-day aesthete, a fin-de-siecle decadent, essentially accusing DeLillo of aestheticizing the political. But as I argue in the previous chapter, although Woods has the terms of what is at stake correct, he inverts them. DeLillo, far from aestheticizing the political, seeks rather to politicize the aesthetic.

By the end of Woods's review it becomes clear that his target is less *Underworld* specifically than what he sees as the larger failure of American postmodern fiction: "DeLillo's struggle with the anaconda of postmodern America . . . is representative of much of American writing since 1960, when Philip Roth famously argued that American reality was more vivid, and hence more fictional, than American fiction. DeLillo is not isolate; where *Underworld* fails, it fails collegiately." Despite its negative assessment, Woods's review, because of its depth and seriousness, is something the student of this novel should not overlook.

An essay that stands between the immediate reviews and the more substantial engagements of academic criticism is Tony Tanner's "Afterthoughts on Don DeLillo's *Underworld*" that appeared in the spring 1998 issue of *Raritan*. In a highly subjective meditation closer to a journalistic review than academic scholarship, Tanner, perhaps the British literary critic most informed about contemporary American fiction, finds *Underworld* a disappointment. He complains that DeLillo's method of disrupting the narrative's chronology is pointless. Although Tanner praises *White Noise* and *Libra*, he feels DeLillo's treatment of paranoia in *Underworld* creates "a rather wearingly uniform paranoid texture" and is little more than "a prolonged and repetitious quoting, or reworking, of Pynchon" (58–59). To his credit, Tanner specifically identifies *Gravity's Rainbow* as the source for DeLillo's repeated "everything is connected" in *Underworld*. But Tanner never seems to consider that the reworking may be DeLillo's critical engagement with Pynchon. Tanner simply sees Pynchon as having already done better what DeLillo wants to do. This comes out again in Tanner's discussion of character in *Underworld*; he complains: "the many voices [in DeLillo's novel] start to seem just part of one, tonally invariant, American Voice. There are hundreds of names in the book, but I would be prepared to bet that . . . none will be remembered six months after reading the novel. As I find, for instance are Pynchon's Stencil and Benny Profane; Oedipa Maas (!); Tyrone Slothrop and Roger Mexico; and — I predict — Mason and Dixon." In sum, Tanner finds that DeLillo's characters, unlike Pynchon's, lack "differentiated consciousnesses" (63). And while willing to grant Pychon forays into the mysterious and inexplicable, Tanner argues that DeLillo is overly concerned with a religious dimension of such mysteries and that *Underworld* "deliquesces into something close to sentimental piety" (70).

Although Tanner's view of *Underworld* is the first to appear in an academic quarterly, it is hardly typical of the novel's reputation in the university, as the following chapter reveals.

4

The Novel's Performance

Almost a year before its publication, *Underworld* was demanding media attention. On October 29, 1996, two days of bidding began over who would publish DeLillo's long-awaited novel, portions of which had appeared in the 1990s in such distinguished venues as *Harper's, Esquire,* and *The New Yorker.* According to *Publisher's Weekly,* Scribner's editor-in-chief Nan Graham purchased the English-language rights to *Underworld* for $1.3 million. (This bid apparently beat offers of $1.5 from both Knopf and Holt for world rights.) Two weeks later, the screen rights to *Underworld* were sold to Scott Rudin of Paramount (a Scribner subsidiary) for an additional million dollars. Rudin is known for his adaptations of novels, most recently Michael Chabon's *Wonder Boys.* Although a treatment of DeLillo's novel is under development, at present there is no immediate plan to produce *Underworld.* Simon and Schuster purchased the audio rights, making *Underworld* the complete media corporate package of Viacom. That DeLillo's novelistic critique of media and multinational capital was itself subject to the machinations of media and multinational capital is an irony of which the author is aware, but as he notes, "Writers write, publishers sell.

That's probably a very old-fashioned conviction but I do maintain it" (Bing, 261). Although aware of the irony, with the large price he received came obligations that the normally reclusive DeLillo previously had avoided — a seven-city book promotional tour, numerous interviews with and profiles by the print media, and even an interview on National Public Radio.

Underworld, a main selection of the Book-of-the-Month Club, made the top ten of *The New York Times Book Review*'s list of bestselling fiction and stayed there for seven weeks from 5 October through 16 November 1997, twice reaching as high as number five, a fact rather remarkable for such a long, complex, and challenging work of fiction. The novel has been translated into German (1998), as well as French and Italian (1999).

Underworld was a finalist for both the 1997 National Book Award and the Pulitzer Prize for fiction, and although it lost to Charles Fraiser's *Cold Mountain* for the former and Philip Roth's *American Pastoral* for the latter, no better indication of the importance of DeLillo's novel in contemporary fiction can be found than the recognition it received on the evening of May 17, 2000. At the annual ceremony of the American Academy of Arts and Letters in New York, DeLillo received the 2000 William Dean Howells Medal for *Underworld*. The award, presented by its 1995 recipient, John Updike, marks what the Academy deems to be "the most distinguished work of American fiction published in the previous five years." As with DeLillo's winning the Jerusalem Prize for his entire career, his peers' honoring him with the Howells Medal once again places *Underworld*'s author in distinguished company. Previous winners include Willa Cather, William Faulkner, William Styron, Thomas Pynchon, and E.L. Doctorow.

Over and above the novel's largely positive reception in its initial reviews, *Underworld* has quickly entered academic discussions of the contemporary novel. In 1999 there were two special issues of journals devoted to DeLillo: *Undercurrent*, an on-line journal, offered "About the Underworld of Don DeLillo," and *Modern Fiction Studies* published "DeLillo II"; each issue featured three essays on *Underworld*. Two of the essays in *Modern Fiction Studies* provide useful correctives to James Wood's reductive assessment in his *New Republic* review (discussed in the previous chapter) centered on DeLillo's poetics.

Timothy L. Parrish's "From Hoover's FBI to Eisenstein's *Unterwelt*: Don DeLillo Directs the Postmodern Novel," argues that, of all the artist figures in *Underworld*, J. Edgar Hoover most closely encodes DeLillo's own narrative poetics. Playing with the meaning of Hoover's title as "Director" of the Federal Bureau of Investigation (in which the position resonates with that of the director of a film), Parrish sees Hoover's ability to make the apparent randomness of contemporary culture cohere in the nascent narratives of his secret files kept on so many Americans. In this regard, Hoover becomes DeLillo's figuration of the consummate theorist-reader-writer of contemporary history. Revising Hoover's politics, though not his aesthetics, DeLillo makes that same randomness of the audio (i.e., the accidental recording of Russ Hodges's broadcast of the 1951 Dodgers-Giants game) and film archive (i.e., the Zapruder film) cohere in his secret history of the Cold War. Also of interest is Philip Nel's " 'A Small Incisive Shock': Modern Forms, Postmodern Politics, and the Role of the Avant-Garde in *Underworld*." This essay positions *Underworld* in a liminal space between modernism and postmodernism. Nel sees DeLillo's faux Eisenstein film, *Unterwelt*, as pointing to the novelist's linguistic refiguration of the photomontage. Relying on the unstable ironies of avant-garde, DeLillo, in Nel's reading, while aware of Fredric Jameson's totalizing version of postmodernism, nevertheless suggests a resistance to the very cultural forces of language and image that his fiction otherwise seems to depict as unassailable.

Similarly, Peter Knight's essay in "DeLillo II" stands as a corrective to the simplistic sense of DeLillo's representation of paranoia in Michael Woods's "Post-Paranoid" that appeared in the *London Review of Books* (See Chapter 3 for a fuller discussion of this review.) In "Everything is Connected: *Underworld*'s Secret History of Paranoia," Knight examines the way DeLillo revises the notion of paranoia from his earlier work. Knight's essay charts the movement from what he calls the secure paranoia of the Cold War to the insecure paranoia of the post-Cold War period.

In addition to this work, Mark Osteen's recent book, *American Magic and Dread: Don DeLillo's Dialogue with Culture* (2000), examines *Underworld* in depth. Reading the novel as an expression of DeLillo's desire to recover the possibility of aesthetic transcendence from the waste of postmodern culture, Osteen's reading complements the interpretation I offer in Chapter 2 and should be considered by anyone working through the novel.

The sophisticated scholarship on *Underworld* in these two journals and in Osteen's book points to a trend in the academic debates on contemporary American fiction. In books published in the last two years, it has practically become de rigueur for the critic, as a matter of credibility, to say something about *Underworld*. And the references to *Underworld* have come in the service of very different kinds of projects. For example, on the one hand Robert Reubein's antitheoretical *Hick's, Tribes, and Dirty Realists: American Fiction after Postmodernism* (2001) concludes with a six-page discussion of *Underworld* that casts DeLillo as a latter-day realist. On the other hand, drawing on Deleuze's and Derrida's discussions of subjectivity and history, Patrick O'Donnell, in the concluding chapter of *Latent Destinies: Cultural Paranoia and Contemporary U.S. Narratives* (2000), contextualizes DeLillo in a postmodern symptomology of paranoia.

Although not a direct indication of *Underworld*'s performance, DeLillo's latest novel, *The Body Artist* (2001) may be read in part as the author's rejoinder to the overwhelming media and academic response to *Underworld*. In some ways the 124-page *Body Artist* with its claustrophobic scope seems the antithesis of *Underworld*. The new novel is restricted to the interior of a house rented by Lauren Hartke, the body artist, who, in the wake of her husband's suicide, attempts to hone her performance of her body into heretofore unimagined erasures of self. Chapter 1 shows us what appears to be a typical morning, though it proves to be the last, of this married couple before Rey Robles, Lauren's husband, drives to his former wife's apartment and kills himself. In the aftermath of Rey's suicide, Lauren, left to pick up the pieces, is haunted by a strange young man with an uncanny ability to repeat things Rey had said. This young man, whom Lauren names Mr. Tuttle, may be real or perhaps is simply her projection.

Although this description suggests that *The Body Artist* has little in common with *Underworld*, the later novel continues DeLillo's meditation on the role of the artist in contemporary society. In fact, the narrative seems to allegorize artistic identity. Rey, who is 64 when he commits suicide, is the same age DeLillo was when he wrote the novel. Rey is also a filmmaker, and given DeLillo's oft-stated identification of his novelistic practice with filmic influences, this bit of character delineation surely invites us to speculate about the degree of self-portraiture that DeLillo allows Rey to bear. The novel presents Rey's obituary and quotes from a film critic who sums up the artist's work: "His subject is people in landscapes of estrangement. He found a spiritual knife-edge in the poetry of alien places, where extreme situations become inevitable and characters are forced toward life-defining moments" (29).

Near the end of the novel, we hear the voice of the critic again, this time through a review of Lauren's performance of the piece she has been working on throughout the narrative. The critic calls Lauren's piece something that disappoints her fans because of its spartan quality that makes it "obscure, slow, difficult and sometimes agonizing" (109) In this metafictional moment, DeLillo's reviewer of Lauren's *Body Time* anticipates the reception of *The Body Artist*, a novel that may disappoint more than a few of DeLillo's fans who expect hip takes on postmodernity. But what we might say is that DeLillo kills off one aspect of his artistic identity (Rey) in order to become Lauren. And the critic's discussion of the way Lauren creates character surely speaks to the similar work of the novelist in creating and inhabiting the voices of many characters. In short, DeLillo responds to his critics, both positive and negative, by appropriating the critic's voice to speak of his continuing quest to imagine a role for the artist in contemporary society. It is in this sense that *The Body Artist* serves almost as an unofficial coda to *Underworld*.

5

Further Reading and Discussion

If you wish to learn more about Don DeLillo, here are two extremely useful websites:

1. Don DeLillo's America — A Don DeLillo Page <http://perival. com/delillo/delillo.html> Established in 1996 by Curt Gardner, this page has a wealth of material on DeLillo's life and art. There is also an extensive bibliography.

2. The Don DeLillo Society Page <http://www.ksu.edu/english/ nelp/delillo/> Maintained by Philip Nel, this is an official organ for the Don DeLillo Society, a group devoted to promoting teaching and scholarship on DeLillo's work. In addition to biography and bibliography, it lists calls for papers for upcoming conferences and collections of essays.

There is also a DeLillo Discussion E-Mail List, run by Cal Godot. Delillo-l is an e-mail forum dedicated to the discussion of DeLillo's literary works. To subscribe to Delillo-l, send an e-mail message to

<Majordomo@jazzflavor.com> with the phrase "subscribe delillo-l"; you will then receive an e-mail with further protocol for this listserv.

DISCUSSION AND PAPER IDEAS

1. As we have seen, DeLillo was very well informed about the historical implications of the specific date that opens the novel. His discussion in "The Power of History" of October 3, 1951, and his linking a famous baseball game to Cold War history suggests a step the engaged reader might take. In Part 5, there are many more dates, since each fragment is headed by a specific date from the 1950s and 1960s.

   Select one or more of these dates, then go to the library and check the microfilm of newspapers from your date(s) to see what links might be made between history and fiction.

2. As noted in chapter 2 of this study, DeLillo seems to construct Pynchon's *The Crying of lot 49* as one of *Underworld's* intertexts. Both novels thematize paranoia and both are concerned with waste and media forms in American consumer culture. To what extent does your reading experience with DeLillo's novel parallel or recall Oeidpa Maas's struggle to make meaning of the Tristero? Oedipa constantly runs up against repeated images but is never certain whether these repetitions are motivated and meaningful or random and arbitrary. For example, "Long Tall Sally," the title of Part 2, refers to a Little Richard song and the nose art on the B-52 that Chuckie Wainwright serves in (and that Klara Sax later paints). But Long Tall Sally is also the name of clothing boutique that Marvin Lundy happens upon in San Francisco. Is this last repetition meaningful in some thematic way in the novel

or does it simply underscore the possibility that not every repetition is meaningful? What other repeated images in *Underworld* resist resolution into clearly motivated patterns?

3. Related to the previous question, despite a similar thematic of paranoia, *The Crying of Lot 49* (1967) was published during the middle of the Cold War. Thirty years later, *Underworld* is a postmortem on the Cold War. What difference, if any, does this historical distance between these two novels make regarding the representation of paranoia?

4. Eric Demming first appears in the novel in Chapter 2 of Part 4 as one of the bombheads with whom Matt Shay works at an underground desert lab in New Mexico. Eric, who seems so assured in the value of his work, tempts Matt into the inner circle of the bombheads even as Matt doubts whether he should continue his work. Later though we see Eric's childhood as one of the fragments of Part 5. What is the effect of this subsequent representation of Eric's adolescence on the reader's perception of the adult Eric?

5. In a novel so concerned with waste, it is interesting that the central symbol is a used baseball, the one Bobby Thomson hit. Why are some select used items valuable (such as sports memorabilia) and enshrined while most others are considered trash and disposed of? What does the ball symbolize to its owners? Does it mean something different, for example, to Charles Wainwright than to Nick Shay?

6. DeLillo has been criticized for the way that his fiction prior to *Underworld* tends to represent white male subjectivity exclusively. In this regard, *Underworld* seems less open to such criticism. What role does the representation of the fragmented histories of women, African-Americans, gays and lesbians, and other marginalized groups have in the novel? Does *Underworld*

still privilege white male subjectivity? If not, what seems more decentered—whiteness or masculinity? To develop your response, you might look closely at a specific character, such as Acey Greenwood, the black lesbian artist and Klara Sax's friend.

7. Consider various representations of art in *Underworld* in relation to the theories of postmodernism articulated by Fredric Jameson and Linda Hutcheon. For Jameson, all contemporary aesthetic production has been placed in the service of commodity production by advertising. Nothing is left but pastiche, the redeployment of previously articulated styles. For Hutcheon, a critical purchase is still available because of contemporary art's parodic relation to the aesthetic past and history. Take a specific instance of aesthetic practice, such as Sabato Rodia's Watts Towers or Acey Greenwood's work on Jayne Mansfield, and discuss whether such art is more complicitous with or critical or the social order.

8. There are numerous minor characters in the novel that have theories of waste. For example, in 1978 Jesse Detwiler, a tenured radical at UCLA and former 1960s anti-war activist, speaks to Nick about the origins of culture as arising out of garbage and suggests turning hidden landfills with dangerous waste into tourist attractions (286–89). Detwiler also is the first to utter the recurring phrase in the novel "Everything is connected," which becomes the narrator's at the novel's conclusion (825–26).

Detwiler, however, is not alone. Viktor Maltsev, a historian in the former Soviet Union turns entrepreneur after the Cold War. Taking Nick to see a novel way to dispose of nuclear waste, Viktor tells Nick that waste is a culture's "secret history" (791). Compare and contrast Jesse's and Viktor's theories of waste. To what extent do you think either of these characters (or others) voice an opinion endorsed by the novel? What, if anything, might make their positions regarding waste untenable?

Appendix—A Synopsis of Part 5

Because Part 5, "Better Things for Better Living through Chemistry" (499–637), gathers so many pieces of different narratives, it is often difficult after an initial reading to find the section one wishes to reexamine. The following provides a brief section-by-section synopsis to help the reader more easily locate material.

CH. 1 (501–12)

November 3, 1952 (501–03)

Nick's view of the juvenile corrections facility in Staatsburg, New York. He wants desperately to believe in the seriousness and purpose of correction system and feels betrayed when a miniature golf course is built for recreation.

October 22, 1962 (504–09)

Lenny Bruce at a club in West Hollywood during the Cuban missile crisis. Lenny's voice is delineated on 506. See also his repeated line: *"We're all gonna die!"* (506, 507, 508)

July 12, 1953 (509–512)

"It was a gesture without history," says Nick, as he thinks about pulling the trigger and the jerk and fall of the body of the man he killed. Nick also thinks about the Alley Boys (black gang members) housed at Staatsburg and their experience the underside of 1950s America.

This is Nick's final weekly appointment with Dr. Lindblad, the psychiatrist at the Staatsburg facility. They talk about Nick's killing and Lindblad relates it to the disappearance of Nick's father. (Note parallels to discussions of other acts of shooting in the novel that are gestures with a history, such as the Zapruder film of the Kennedy assassination and the Texas Highway Killer video.)

Nick is then sent to the Jesuit's extension program run by Fordham University "somewhere near a lake in Minnesota."

CH. 2 (513–35)

October 8, 1957 (513–21)

The Demming family in suburbia. Here DeLillo explores the new language that emerged in consumer culture to describe the suburban lifestyle.

Everything is marked as typical but this is a day with Cold-War implications since the Russian Sputnik satellite is visible in the night sky.

August 14, 1964 (521–26)

An African-American speaker exhorts Civil Rights protesters at a sit-in at the whites only section of the Greyhound terminal in Jackson, MS. Thomson's bat has been replaced by the cop's billy clubs.

Cotter Martin's sister, Rosie, has come down from New York to participate. Non-violence turns violent in the National Guard response to the demonstration. Note the parallels between this crowd and the one that opens the novel in the prologue.

December 19, 1961 (526–35)

Charles Wainwright, a Madison Avenue account supervisor, develops an advertisement for orange juice. Thinking about his strained relationship with his son, Wainwright decides to give the Thomson ball to his son, Chuckie.

CH. 3 (536–554)

January 11, 1955 (536–43)

Nick visits Father Palus, who becomes Nick's new ideological father. Father's "confession" to Nick. They work through the names of the parts of a shoe.

October 24, 1962 (544–48)

Lenny plays a club in San Francisco. Once again, DeLillo is fascinated with the effects of Bruce's ability to ventriloquize the voices of culture.

June 14, 1957 (548–554)

Nick's trip west with Amy that marks the end of their relationship.

November 28, 1966 (555–65)

J. Edgar Hoover and Clyde Tolson at the Waldorf preparing for Truman Capote's Black and White Ball. Clyde tells Hoover that garbage guerrilla's plan to steal Hoover's garbage and turn it into performance art.

Tanya Berenger fits Edgar's mask for the ball that turns him into "a butch biker." The chapter emphasizes the clear yet unconsummated homoeroticism of Edgar and Clyde's relationship.

January 19, 1967 (565–67)

As do all the other student nurses with whom she lives, Janet Urbaniak (Matt Shay's future wife) runs from the hospital through an urban wasteland to her apartment complex.

November 29, 1966 (567–579)

Edgar and Clyde attend the Black and White Ball. Despite Clyde's best efforts, a suspicious Volkswagen beetle with a psychedelic paint job follows them from dinner to the party. In the mixture of famous people from various levels of society at the ball, Clyde senses a dangerous destabilization in that very mix that could challenge cultural hierarchy.

At Edgar's urging, Clyde asks a young woman in a raven's mask to dance. She knows who he is; as they dance, she critiques the

Establishment. Suddenly she joins a group of other raven masked women, nuns, and skeleton men; together they form a troupe that performs a dance that mocks the Black and White Ball. This scene invokes a different Edgar—Edgar Allan Poe and his story "The Masque of the Red Death"

CH. 5 (580–595)

October 25, 1962 (580–86)

Lenny plays to a packed house in Chicago. He places a condom on his tongue and does a bit about Saran Wrap as an alternative form of birth control. The chapter meditates on the power of forbidden words.

July 2, 1959 (587–89)

Nick takes Amy to get an abortion in Mexico.

October 27, 1962 (590–95)

Lenny in Miami does a bit about the names of the US leaders and the implications of their WASPish identities.

CH. 6 (596–616)

October 18, 1967 (596–604)

Marian Bowman (Nick's future wife) visits home in Madison, Wisconsin. It is a day of student protests at the University of Wisconsin against the Vietnam War and the military-industrial complex focused on Dow Chemical's recruitment on campus. The voice on the radio satirizes the advertising slogans of several chemical companies. (Note the presence of the Day-Glow VW and the street theater, which suggests that the same people who disrupt the Black and White Ball were previously in Madison.)

Marion calls Nick and tells him she wants to get married; he does not answer.

February 6, 1953 (605–06)

Matt still at home while Nick is Upstate in correction.

December 1, 1969 (606–16)

Chuckie Wainwright, navigator, flying a mission in Vietnam in a B-52 with the Long Tall Sally nose art. (The same plane later becomes part of Klara Sax's art project.) Chuckie talks with Louis T. Bakey, an African-American fellow crewman on the B-52. Louis gives a chilling description of his earlier participation in a military test to see the effects of an atomic blast on the crew of a B-52.

November 9, 1965 (617–23)

Set on the day of the power blackout that plunged a major portion of the East Coast in darkness, Nick, who has recently met Marian, runs into a childhood acquaintance, Jerry, at a seedy bar on New York's Lower East Side. Jerry wants to make an evening of it and suggests a trip to their old haunts in the Bronx, but Nick only wants to escape.

October 29, 1962 (623–33)

Lenny in NYC playing to 3000 people in Carnegie Hall at the conclusion of the Cuban missile crisis. Lenny starts doing the voice of the black street preacher and cannot seem to stop. He starts to tell a dirty joke about a girl who can blow smoke rings with her vagina but interrupts this narrative to begin the story of Esmeralda, who is not yet born.

November 9, 1965 (631–37)

This final fragment picks up from the thread from p. 623, continuing the story of Nick during the NYC blackout. As he walks along, Nick thinks maybe Jerry was right about a trip to the Bronx but decides finally to returns to hotel, where he pointedly does not call Marian in order to contemplate his loneliness and distance from his youth.

Bibliography

Works by Don DeLillo

Fiction

Americana. Boston: Houghton Mifflin, 1971.
End Zone. Boston: Houghton Mifflin, 1972.
Great Jones Street. Boston: Houghton Mifflin, 1973.
Ratner's Star. New York: Knopf, 1976.
Players. New York: Knopf, 1977.
Running Dog. New York: Knopf, 1978.
The Names. New York: Knopf, 1982.
White Noise. New York: Viking, 1985.
Libra. New York: Viking, 1988.
Mao II. New York: Viking, 1991.
Underworld. New York: Scribner, 1997.
The Body Artist. New York: Scribner, 2001.

Essay

"The Power of History." *New York Times Magazine* 7 Sept. 1997: 60–63.

Reviews of *Underworld*

Note: Many of the reviews, profiles, and interviews are available electronically through the Lexis-Nexis Academic Universe database.

Amis, Martin. "Survivors of the Cold War." 5 Oct. 1997, 16 Jan. 2001 <http://www.nytimes.com/books/97/10/05/reviews/971005.05amisdt. html.>.

Battsby, Eileen. "Pitched into the Future." *Irish Times*. 10 Jan. 1998: 68.

Bigsby, Christopher. "The Country Where History is More Inventive than Fiction." London *Telegraph*. 3 Jan. 1998.

Caldwell, Gail. "Blasts from the Past." *Boston Globe*. 28 Sept. 1997: F1.

Didbin, Michael. "Out to Get Us" *Sunday London Times*. 4 Jan. 1998.

Kakutani, Michiko. "Of American as a Splendid Junk Heap." *New York Times*. 16 Sept. 1997. Late Edition: E1.

Leonard, John. "American Jitters." *The Nation*. 3 Nov. 1997, 16 Jan. 2001 <http://past.thenation.com/issue/971103/1103leon.html>

Marchand, Philip. "When Garbage and Paranoia Rule." *Toronto Star*. 4 Oct. 1997: M17.

Morrison, Blake. "A Big Hit Strikes it Lucky." *London Independent*. 4 Jan. 1998: Features 24.

O'Hagan, Andrew. "Don DeLillo Gets under America's Skin." *Voice Literary Supplement*. 16 Oct. 1997: 8.

Pyper, Andrew. "Inside the Volcano." *Montreal Gazette*. 18 Oct. 1998: Books 13.

Sante, Luc. "Between Hell and History." *New York Review of Books*. 6 Nov. 1997: 4–7. 16 Jan. 2001 <http://www.nybooks.com/nyrev/WWWarch-display.cgi?19971106004R>.

Tanner, Tony. "Afterthoughts on Don DeLillo's *Underworld*." *Raritan*. 17.4 (1998): 48–71.

Wiegand, David. "We Are What We Waste." *San Francisco Chronicle*. 21 Sept. 1997: Book Review 1, 6.

Wood, Michael. "Post-Paranoid." *London Review of Books*. 5 Feb. 1998, 16 Jan. 2001 <http//www.lrb.co.uk/v20n03/wood0119.html>.

Woods, James. "Black Noise." *The New Republic.* 10 Nov. 1997, 16 Jan. 2001 <wysiwyg://68/http://magazines.enew . . . /archive/11/111097/wood111097.html?>

Interviews and Profiles

Begley, Adam. "Don DeLillo: The Art of Fiction CXXXV." *Paris Review.* 35:128 (Fall 1993): 274–306.

Bing, Jonathan. "The Ascendance of Don DeLillo." *Publisher's Weekly.* 11 Aug. 1997. 261–263.

DeCurtis, Anthony. "An Outsider in This Society: An Interview with Don DeLillo." *Introducing Don DeLillo.* Ed. Frank Lentricchia. Durham: Duke UP, 1991. 43–66.

Echlin, Kim. "Baseball and the Cold War." *Ottawa Citizen.* 28 Dec. 1997: E5.

Goldstein, William. "PW Interviews." *Publishers Weekly.* 19 Aug. 1988. 55–56.

Harris, Robert R. "A Talk with Don DeLillo." *New York Times Book Review.* 10 Oct. 1982: 26.

LeClair, Tom. "An Interview with Don DeLillo." *Contemporary Literature.* 23 (1982): 19–31.

Passaro, Vince. "Dangerous Don DeLillo." *New York Times Magazine.* 19 May 1991: 36–38, 76–77. 20 Feb. 2001. <http://www.nytimes.com/books/97/03/16/lifetimes/del-v-dangerous.html.>

Rothstein, Mervyn. "A Novelist Faces His Themes on New Ground." *New York Times.* 20 Dec. 1987, Sec. 2: 5, 19.

Williams, Richard. "Everything under the Bomb." *London Guardian.* 10 Jan. 1998, 16 Jan. 2001 <http://books.guardian.co.uk/reviews/generalfiction/0,6121,96812,00.html>.

Secondary Materials

19th Jerusalem International Book Fair Home Page. 20 May 1999. <http://www.jerusalembookfair.com/page6.html>.

Aaron, Daniel. "How to Read Don DeLillo." *Introducing Don DeLillo*. Ed. Frank Lentricchia. Durham: Duke UP, 1991. 67–82.

Baudrillard, Jean. *Simulations*. Trans. Paul Foss, et al. New York: Semiotext(e), 1983.

Benjamin, Walter. "The Work of Art in the Age of Mechanical Reproduction." *Illuminations*. New York: Harcourt, 1955. 219–253.

Fitzgerald, F. Scott. *The Great Gatsby*. New York: Scribner's, 1925.

Gentry, Curt. *J. Edgar Hoover: The Man and His Secrets*. New York: Norton, 1991.

Hutcheon, Linda. *The Politics of Postmodernism*. New York: Routledge, 1989.

Jameson, Fredric. *Postmodernism, or, The Cultural Logic of Late Capitalism*. Durham: Duke UP, 1991.

Knight, Peter. "Everything is Connected: *Underworld*'s Secret History of Paranoia." *Modern Fiction Studies*. 45 (1999): 811–36.

Nel, Philip. " 'A Small Incisive Shock': Modern Forms, Postmodern Politics, and the Role of the Avant-Garde in *Underworld*." *Modern Fiction Studies*. 45 (1999): 724–52.

O'Donnell, Patrick. *Latent Destinies: Cultural Paranoia and Contemporary U.S. Narratives*. Durham: Duke UP, 2000.

Osteen, Mark. *American Magic and Dread: Don DeLillo's Dialogue with Culture*. Philadelphia: U of Pennsylvania P, 2000.

Parish, Timothy L. "From Hoover's FBI to Eisenstein's *Untervelt*: DeLillo Directs the Postmodern Novel." *Modern Fiction Studies*. 45 (1999): 696–723.

Passaro, Vince. "Don DeLillo and the Towers." 2 Oct. 2001 <http://www.mrbellersneighborhood.com/sec5/wtcdelillo.html>

Pynchon, Thomas. *The Crying of Lot 49*. 1966. New York: Perennial, 1986.

Reubein, Robert. *Hicks, Tribes, and Dirty Realists: American Fiction after Postmodenism*. Lexington: U of Kentucky P, 2001.

Rogin, Michael. *Ronald Reagan, the Movie*. Berkeley: U of California P, 1987.